PET LOSS
AND DIVINE
HEALING

A COMPASSIONATE GUIDE FOR
NAVIGATING YOUR DEVASTATING LOSS

RACHEL SHIRLEY

Cover Artwork by @_.augustosilva._
Interior formatting by KUHN Design Group | kuhndesigngroup.com

Disclaimer: The content of this book is provided for informational purposes only and is intended to support, not replace, the relationship between a person and their existing healthcare provider. While I aim to provide guidance and support for those grieving the loss of a pet, it's essential to acknowledge that this book does not offer medical or psychological advice. Please consult your healthcare provider if you require professional medical or psychological assistance.

Furthermore, if you find yourself in a crisis or if you are contemplating hurting yourself or others, please reach out for help immediately. The National Suicide Prevention Lifeline is available 24/7 and can be reached at 1-800-273-TALK (1-800-273-8255). There are people who want to listen and who can help you navigate through this difficult time. Remember, you are not alone, and support is available to you.

By reading this book, you acknowledge that the author and publisher are not liable for any harm or damage arising from your actions or decisions. This disclaimer is not intended to negate the support and assistance this book may provide but to remind readers of the importance of seeking appropriate professional help when needed.

To the world's devoted and dedicated pet parents—both present and those yet to embark on the incredible journey of companionship—this book is for you. It will always be one of my most treasured purpose-driven missions here on earth from my heart to yours.

To the friends and family of pet lovers, thank you for supporting the pet lovers in your life with compassion, empathy, and grace as they embark on one of the most challenging losses of their lives. You are not only equipping them with the words in this book to help heal their heart, you are also showing them they are not alone, and for that, I am grateful.

And last but not least, to my beloved clients, thank you for allowing me the honor to support you along your grief and healing journey. I dedicate this book to you, too, as our meaningful conversations have impacted my heart and inspired me to keep on keeping on. For that, I am grateful.

CONTENTS

CHAPTER FOUR: TAKING CARE OF YOUR BROKEN HEART

CHAPTER FIVE: TAKING CARE OF YOUR BODY EVEN IN DEEP SORROW

CHAPTER SIX: NAVIGATING RELATIONSHIPS WHILE GRIEVING

CHAPTER SEVEN:
ADJUSTING TO A NEW NORMAL

CHAPTER EIGHT:
PAYING IT FORWARD (LEGACY)

CHAPTER NINE:
TIME TO LOVE AGAIN

CHAPTER TEN: FOR THOSE WHO...

CHAPTER ELEVEN: CLIENT
STORIES IN THEIR OWN WORDS

INTRODUCTION

During my workday from home, I received a traumatic and heart-wrenching phone call from my husband and our vet. As I picked up the phone, I was not expecting to hear what I did about our beloved boxer, Winston.

"I'm sorry to tell you this, but Winston has a brain tumor and cancer all over his body. It is probably best to have his peaceful passing as soon as possible to relieve his suffering."

What? I felt like the world had suddenly caved in, and I was suffocating. I knew something was wrong with Winston, but when I took him in to be checked out, I never imagined this diagnosis or an outcome that was so final.

I had a hunch he might have cancer, but it never crossed my mind for one second that we wouldn't have more time to love on him and spoil him. He was only nine years old and about to leave this earth, taking our shattered hearts with him.

It was devastating and completely unbelievable that this was our reality.

As you can imagine, it felt like my heart dropped right out of my body as my breathing became labored with fear, confusion, and deep sorrow.

I know you have picked up this book because you (or someone you love) can relate in some way, whether your sweet ones had a sudden diagnosis or a terminal illness, were in a tragic accident, needed compassionate euthanasia to end their suffering, or passed when you were not there with them as they took their final breath.

My heart is with you, my beloved new friend.

While I'm not a therapist or counselor, I am a certified professional coach, helping families and clients feel heard, understood, and supported through their grief and healing journey. It truly is an honor and privilege to support you and other pet parents in this meaningful and significant way.

From my personal grief experiences and those of the precious families and clients that I'm blessed to work with daily, I intimately understand and profoundly know your pain, despair, confusion, grief, and deep sorrow.

Being certified as a professional coach and a pet loss grief coach brings divine purpose, meaning, and significance into my life. It's what became the catalyst for my decision to write this book. I feel passionate about walking the journey with those of you who are agonizing over the loss of your sweet one, too.

As God placed this book in my spirit, countless clients were asking me to write a book. It was a delightful confirmation of what I had been sensing: This world needs to know there is healing, hope, and harmony to embrace through pet loss.

I intentionally wrote and designed this book with you in mind. Please see this devotional book as love letters written from my heart to yours.

Because I understand this grief is more brutal than we can imagine, I did some of the heavy lifting for you. I know reading a long and complicated book is the last thing on your agenda. You've got enough to think about, and your energy levels are probably nearly depleted from grieving. Because of this, I wrote several short love letters to you on different topics that I hope will be valuable for you along the way.

Throughout this book, you'll find "Rachel's Reflections and Reminders" at the end of each love letter for you to grab and go to when needed. I know that sometimes it's hard to read and concentrate, so those reflections and reminders are there if you just need something topical and easy to consume and chew on for the day.

I've also added a few client stories in their own words to show that what you are experiencing right now is normal and a natural part of the grieving and healing process. I hope they bring you a sense of identity and comfort in the fact that you are not alone.

Throughout this book, I will invite you to consider perspectives and themes of grief that you may be familiar with, may have forgotten, may need a gentle reminder about, or might not have heard before.

One of the most significant themes for you to contemplate will be that you will see your sweet one again in heaven. Another is that our beautiful and precious pets are on loan to care for until God calls them home to heaven; they are not our possessions.

They are one of the most precious gifts from our Creator. Yes! The one who created you and loves you more than you know, and He loves to bless you with beautiful and priceless gifts—like your sweet one.

So, my friend, let's unite our hearts and embrace your grief and divine healing journey with grace and grit. I promise you will get through this moment in time if you bring an open heart, sound mind, and the willingness to invite God's divine peace and healing to your tired and tender heart. I'm with you and for you, beloved friend.

Let the journey of healing begin.

From my heart to yours,

Rachel

CHAPTER ONE

YOU WILL
SEE YOUR SWEET
ONE AGAIN
IN HEAVEN

As much as it is a great honor to pour my experience, strength,
and hope onto these pages as a love letter from my heart to yours,
I equally understand the gravity of what you have been through.

You're likely reading this because you or someone you
love has experienced one of the most significant losses in life.
Let me be one of the first to let you know you are not alone.
And I have some delightful news for you;
I believe you will see your beloved pet again in heaven!

1.1

YOUR PET IS STILL BEING CARED FOR TODAY

Your love, Lord, reaches to the heavens, your faithfulness to
the skies. Your righteousness is like the highest mountains,
your justice like the great deep. You, Lord, preserve both
people and animals. How priceless is your unfailing love,
O God! People take refuge in the shadow of your wings.

PSALM 36:5–8

How could Winston be gone from earth? And where? Where is he? Is he in heaven? Will I see him again?

These are some questions I wrestled with when my sweet boy Winston passed. Since then, my clients have asked me these questions, or a variation of them, on a daily basis.

So, as I share with them, and now you too, it's my honor and privilege to sit quietly with you as you contemplate the mystery and unfamiliarity of these questions about death.

As I mentioned in the introduction of this book, I am not a therapist, pastor, or even someone who claims to have all the answers.

However, I can share a genuine and confirming belief in the goodness and kindness of our Creator and a passionate heart to walk alongside you as you wrestle with these critical questions too.

You may have lost faith in God and His goodness or not believe in God at all. That's okay. He knows your heart and cares for you deeply. As much as it may feel this way, He is not upset with you, nor is he punishing you.

I invite you to set down any self-judgment you may have about your faith journey. Then, I invite you to be open to how God may want to speak to you through losing your beloved pet.

Our Heavenly Father, who created you and me, also created your beloved pet. I believe He is a loving Father, continuing to care for your sweet one in heaven.

Your beloved pet's death was more than likely caused by disease or a tragic accident caused by human error. Whatever the reason, I won't pretend to be able to explain why bad things happen to good people and innocent pets. That is way above my pay grade; it's God's business, not mine.

My business is how I interpret and respond to these challenging questions. When they swirl around in my or my client's overly-exhausted mind, I ask, "Is this thought helpful or harmful?"

For example, here are questions for you to contemplate: Is it helpful or harmful to believe you will never see your pet again, and what you experienced was just a moment in time that will never happen again? Is it helpful or harmful to believe that your relationship with your sweet one was worth every ounce of grief and sorrow you are experiencing now because you will be reunited one day?

Think about it.

When we said yes to welcoming our pets into our hearts and homes, we received the most incredible gift and the purest form of love on earth. Although our beloved pets' physical bodies are no longer with us here on earth, their spirits are with us, and you can choose to believe you will see them in heaven.

The timing of when you move from earth to heaven is up to God, but until you are reunited with your pet in heaven, you can have peace in your heart, knowing God is taking care of them and they are closer than you think.

I believe what you thought was the end—their physical body no longer with you—is not the end.

Your love story continues as you honor their legacy, live out the lessons they taught you, and live your life full of purpose, knowing your love was and still is worth it.

You cared for them well. Now it's God's turn. I believe you will be reunited, and until then, your new purpose is to represent their sweet kindness and exuberant love here on earth until you meet again.

Beloved friend, I encourage you to invite peace and a new sense of purpose into your broken and tender heart. Decide today to illuminate your sweet one's love throughout your daily life because they are with you in spirit.

Your questions are a normal response to the grief you are experiencing, but as you embark on this grief journey, try to celebrate the good news of your sweet one's continued care and a delightful reunion ahead.

Your love story with them never dies.

Losing a beloved pet can be a profoundly emotional and challenging experience. Remember to embrace an open mind, hold on to hope, and find solace in the belief of a reunion in the afterlife.

Each individual's grief journey is unique, and finding comfort and healing may come from different sources, beliefs, or practices.

The most important thing is to give yourself the time and space to process your emotions and memories and to seek support from those who understand and care.

RACHEL'S REFLECTIONS & REMINDERS

1. Death can be a challenging and unfamiliar concept to understand, and it's okay to wrestle with questions and emotions related to it.

2. Whether you have faith in God, have lost·your faith, or don't believe in God at all, it's okay. Allow yourself to be on your unique faith journey without self-judgment.

3. Having faith and believing in a loving Creator who cares for humans and their beloved pets can bring peace, purpose, and hope to your broken heart.

4. Invite peace into your grieving heart and find a new purpose by honoring your pet's legacy and embodying the love they shared with you.

5. Remember that your love story with your pet doesn't end with their physical absence; it continues to shape your life.

THE BIG PICTURE—ACCEPT THEY WERE ON LOAN

*The earth is the Lord's, and everything in
it, the world, and all who live in it;*

PSALM 24:1

It's easy to live in the world we do today and feel as though the things we have acquired belong to us. Logic says if you work hard for something and purchase it, it's yours. Logic says if you train hard or study enough, success is yours. If you put your hand to it, it's yours to do with as you please.

We buy things, trade things to upgrade, and sell things that are no longer needed or serving their intended purpose. It makes perfect sense, right? After all, this is how the world's economy works. And frankly, we are blessed to have the opportunity to own possessions that make our lives more enjoyable and function well.

There's just one caveat. How we view these wonderful possessions makes a difference in the condition of our outer and inner lives. The world may tell us that the possessions we own, lease, rent, buy, and sell are under our ownership. This is partly true and partly false. Yes, we have them in our possession, but the true owner is the Creator, our Heavenly Father. He created you, me, and everything here on earth, and as Creator and Owner, He has loaned everything we have to us for a time.

We are here on this planet, just passing through, and the things we get to enjoy are temporarily ours. This is one of the spiritual laws of life. God created the earth and entrusts you with many possessions, relationships, and responsibilities. This is a stewardship issue that I'm hoping and praying you might explore for yourself if it's a new concept or something you've rejected in the past.

I can tell you this and mean it as gently as possible: your sweet one was on loan, my love.

Even though we may have felt that they were ours, they were on loan from the One who created them. Our Heavenly Father knew you would love and appreciate such a joy-filled bundle of love to help bring you joy while here on earth. He gave you your sweet one to help you not feel alone when you go through the trials and troubles in life and for the times of celebrating new milestones on your journey.

He created your sweet one and gave them as a gift to you because He loves you. He entrusted you with them because He knew you would cherish them. And He did all this because He delights in blessing you in this life and for eternity.

God is good, and He is *your* Father. The term "father" may have a negative connotation if you didn't have a healthy relationship with your earthly father, but I can assure you that God is unlike your earthly father.

We, humans, fail one another, but God the Father is full of love, compassion, gentleness, forgiveness, grace, patience, and so many other wonderful attributes. He's a good Father and loves you unconditionally, so He loves giving you good gifts—like your sweet one.

Everything we have in this life and the afterlife is a gift from God. Our relationships, jobs, animals, possessions, and eternal security, to name a few, it's all from Him. We are here on earth now simply to be good stewards of these incredible gifts and the promise of those to come.

We have the option to focus on the good things we have or the things we wish we had but lack. One choice speaks life, and the other speaks death.

Choose life over death, my friend. If you are focused entirely on the loss of your pet instead of the joy you experienced when you had them, you may miss out on the peace of mind and perspective God wants you to have on this journey.

I know it's hard to manage, but I encourage you to take an inventory of your perspective about what we have here on this earth and try to look for the good around you, even as you are mourning, grieving, and healing your heart. God knows what He is doing, and He knows what we need. He won't keep what is meant for us away from us.

Become open-minded and willing to invite this perspective into your spirit, then watch how He takes great care of you! Life is so fun when you are waiting with great anticipation for the beautiful gifts God will continue to bless you with throughout your life. And also, watch what happens when you share this newfound secret to enjoying your life here on earth with those you love. Your life will change, and so will the lives of others, as you all become better versions of yourselves as intended by our Heavenly Father.

I asked my husband, Simon when he first heard about this principle of stewardship and everything on loan. After much reflection and contemplation, he said, "It was when you taught it to me, Rachel. Wow! That means I didn't learn this until my late fifties." Simon continued, "And understanding the principle of stewardship—that things are on loan to me in this life—has changed my life and outlook on stuff. I now have freedom from thinking that possessions are more important than they are. Because of this, I prioritize relationships with more significance because I will see the people and pets I have had a relationship with in heaven, and my possessions will not go with me."

Well, talk about feeling humbled and honored. I definitely was, but I was especially moved by my husband's outlook on possessions and priorities. He got it right. Our possessions will not go with us after this life, but we can invest in the things that will—the people and pets that matter to our hearts.

I hope this concept lands in your heart and sits there, too.

I don't have it all figured out, and I don't get it all right, but I've positioned my heart to continue learning about stewardship and yielding to God in the areas I struggle to surrender.

We can all grow in this, right?

Please give this some consideration in light of your grief. Your sweet one really is on loan for a season. When you adopt this perspective, God's Spirit brings you more profound understanding and peace in your loss.

RACHEL'S REFLECTIONS & REMINDERS

1. Understand that while you may possess things and build relationships, the true owner of all is God, who has entrusted these gifts to you for a time.

2. Embrace a perspective of gratitude and contentment for the blessings God has given you, from relationships and possessions to eternal security.

3. Focus on the joys and positive experiences you had with your sweet one rather than dwelling solely on their loss. Embrace life and the gifts that come your way.

4. Be open to inviting the perspective of stewardship into your spirit, then watch how it brings joy and anticipation for the gifts God has in store for your life.

5. Prioritize relationships over material possessions, recognizing that the people and pets you love will have an eternal impact beyond this life.

LET GO AND TRUST GOD

*All the things in this world are gifts of God, created for
us, to be the means by which we can come to know him
better, love him more surely, and serve him more faithfully.*

JAMES W. SKEHAN[1]

You can steward your time (work time, home time, relationship time, self-care time, fun time, etc.), talent (skills and abilities for jobs, volunteering, causes, etc.), and treasures (money and possessions) to build your kingdom here on Earth, or you can steward them for God's Kingdom.

Your own kingdom is likely focused inward, on yourself. This creates a *me, myself, and I* syndrome that constantly asks, "How can I get more stuff? How can I attain more accolades and more recognition?" Or maybe it's more relationships that matter to the world, along with more success, so you feel important or significant. It also can be that we desire more alcohol, sex, pills, food, or work (you choose your go-to) so that we can feel better about ourselves. The key word here is *ourselves.*

A Kingdom-of-God perspective is others-focused, and it asks, "How can I give my time, talents, and treasures to help others be their best? How can I help others become all they are meant to be? What do I need to do or sacrifice to put others first?"

See the difference?

It's about worshiping the One who created us rather than worshiping the things of the world that, if we are honest, we know don't bring us peace, joy, or comfort. We can chase them, but we will just feel unsatisfied.

Ultimately, this pursuit takes us further and further away from God's design and intent for us: to trust Him for what we need and with what we already have.

When you have a heavenly perspective that's open-handed with what God gives you, it makes it much easier when He deems it fit to take it away for a time.

Man, I'll tell you that when you see your pet as a gift on loan, there is great freedom in knowing you were a good steward to your sweet one, the gift God gave you to enjoy for a season.

Remember, you and I—and our sweet ones—have expiration dates. God's timing on when it's time for His created ones to go home to be with Him is completely up to Him. He knows what is best, and we can trust that He will also do what is best for us.

So, if you can get to the point that you believe this about God, does it make it a little easier not to get upset with Him when we go through loss?

We don't always have to understand why now, but we can respect that He knows why and loves us. Remember that He gave you a wonderful gift, which you will get to see again. And also, take hold of the fact that you can have more pets in your lifetime if you and God desire that and He wills it to be.

The death of our pets is an opportunity to live with open hands and detach in love when it's time. When we hold on too tightly, it invites unhealthy thoughts, words, and actions to come through us in our anger and grief. In turn, this causes more trauma, turmoil, treachery, and trouble than any of us need.

Let them go, my friend.

Perhaps you are holding on to the past because you are scared of what you will feel or experience if you do let go of them. Please know that for whatever all-knowing reason God had for taking them, you *will* get through this.

I invite you to face your fears and let go of the anxiety and denial that no longer serves who you are meant to become.

I know that's a lot to take in. Take a moment to calm your thoughts. And now, take a few deep breaths to ground yourself emotionally.

I love you, even if we've never met.

I care for you, your spirit, your wellness, your mental strength, the condition of your heart, your family and other relationships, your dreams, your visions of what can be, and most of all, I care about your eternity. I care about all of you. And I want what is best for you, so please don't think that I expect you to, or think you should, think like I do. I don't. I want you to think for yourself about the pivotal point your life is in right now.

Grief can bring us to our knees. And while that feels impossibly hard, it's the best place to be because it allows us to come to the end of ourselves, where God will faithfully meet us in His love. He will renew our minds, hearts, strength, perseverance, determination, and grit so we can move forward with grace, self-compassion, humility, mercy, and loving-kindness toward ourselves as we heal from this devastating loss.

The enemy of your soul wants you to focus on and strive after stuff, while the One who created you wants you to recognize that He is the giver of your gifts, and He wants you to hold them with high regard and a deeper level of appreciation and value.

Everything is on loan. It is an honor and privilege to be a good steward of everything in our lives, knowing that they are not our possessions, so we don't have to hold on so tightly.

So, the next time someone asks you why God took them away, you can confidently say, "I don't understand everything, but I do know my beloved pet was His to begin with, and He trusted me enough to enjoy them while here on earth. He used my sweet one to help me learn some of the most incredible and valuable lessons about unconditional love, patience, forgiveness, loyalty, and fun that I will carry on throughout my life. And I'm sad, but I can live freely knowing I did my best to care for them while they were mine."

Now, that's freedom if I've ever heard it.

Beloved, thank you for allowing me to speak freely and straight from my heart to yours.

In your grief journey, hold onto the knowledge that your sweet one was a precious gift from God, and their love and impact on your life will always be cherished.

Embrace the concept of stewardship by opening your hands and focusing on living a life of purpose, love, and service, knowing that the best is yet to come.

Allow God's love and grace to guide you as you heal, and remember that you are not alone in this journey. Trust that, in time, you will find peace, hope, purpose, and comfort in the promise of a beautiful reunion with your beloved pet in heaven.

RACHEL'S REFLECTIONS & REMINDERS

1. Recognize that everything in our lives, including our beloved pets, is on loan from our Heavenly Father. Embrace the concept of stewardship and appreciate the gifts we are entrusted with.

2. Shift your perspective to move away from the mindset of ownership and materialism to focus on valuing our relationships and experiences in this life.

3. Treasure the time and love you shared with your beloved pet as a beautiful gift from God. Find comfort in knowing that they were given to you out of love.

4. Allow grief to bring you to your knees, opening the door to renewed perspectives, resilience, and personal growth.

5. Recognize that holding on too tightly to possessions or relationships can lead to unnecessary pain and turmoil. Embrace the art of letting go with grace and self-compassion.

1.4

YOU WILL SEE YOUR SWEET ONE IN HEAVEN AGAIN

Christ died for animals indirectly because his death for humanity purchased redemption for what was brought down by humanity's sin, including animals.

RANDY ALCORN[2]

What a tremendous honor and pleasure it is to be on this journey with you. The good news is that if we don't get a chance to meet in person here on earth, we will meet in heaven one day, celebrating our new life with our sweet ones. I look forward to that day, my beloved friend!

For those who believe in heaven and know it is real, keep shining your light as you wait until our Father brings you home and reunites you with your sweet one (or multiple sweet ones) in our eternal life. And enjoy the many more heavenly treasures and sweet ones He sends you from heaven while you are here!

Here's what I'll share for those who have questions and are unsure about our Father, the Creator, and heaven.

You are right where you need to be.

I understand this book is about pet loss and pet loss grief, so it might feel confusing that I talk about heaven a lot here. But the truth is, I would not be doing *all* I can to help you if I did not explain a little more about heaven.

You could turn this page right now, and we will definitely still be friends. I do not take any offense if you would rather not keep reading, my love.

I want you to know that having questions and uncertainty is okay. I understand that, and I felt the same way. I was once skeptical about the Bible. In fact, I told a group of new-to-church people like me that I was actually scared of the Bible.

I remember the moment like it was yesterday, yet it was many years ago. We were in a small group together called Starting Point at North Point Community Church in Alpharetta, Georgia, when I dropped that bomb. I felt nervous sharing my truth, but I quickly learned that I was part of a beautiful group of people who also had questions about this whole God thing.

The small group leader looked at me, bringing her big Bible close to her heart, and said, "Rachel, this is the Word of God. He created this as a love letter to you and me. He gives us hope and guides us as He shows us through His Word how to live extraordinary lives. He is your Heavenly Father, and you can trust Him and His Word."

A warm sensation that was practically indescribable came over me. I knew I was home. I knew it was a safe place to share my skeptical thoughts and to let go of my shame in having doubts about the God of the universe.

I was free to be me as I learned more about the Father I knew I had but had never really known. You see, I loved God; I was just scared of Him and the Bible. Praise God that I gathered the courage to find the truth for myself that day.

Now, I'm going to give you some things to consider about heaven and seeing your pet there again, and I want you to know that I am not trying to convince you of anything. You and your faith—or lack of faith—are your business. But, I am thankful for the opportunity to share with you what I believe about our beloved pets being in heaven waiting for us. Let me just preface by saying I am not a pastor, Bible scholar, or theologian. However, I am a faith-filled woman of God who loves Jesus, so I feel equipped to give you a few truths and resources to review for yourself.

I believe in teaching others what I can and leaving the convincing up to God.

First, God created the earth, humans, and all creatures (see the creation account in Gen. 1–2). God mentions animals throughout the Bible, showing how people and animals, as well as the relationships between them, are important to Him.

As we see throughout history and today, God's character can be trusted.

We can trust that He will make the earth, humans, and animals new again because He said He will (2 Pet. 3:13).

So, with that being said, one of my favorite books on heaven, where you can find a few chapters speaking about animals and our pets in heaven, is *Heaven* by Randy Alcorn.

This is a must-read book. It changed my life; I pray it will do the same for you.

As I mentioned in the introduction to this book, I have a list on my website, www.rachel-shirley.com, with "Rachel's Favorites," where I have included other resources and a few YouTube videos on the subject matter that I often share with my clients, and boy do they love them as much as I do!

RACHEL'S REFLECTIONS & REMINDERS

1. Embrace the hope and belief that you will be reunited with your beloved pet in heaven. Trust in the promise of an eternal and joyful reunion.

2. If you have questions or doubts about faith and the concept of heaven, be open to seeking understanding through resources, discussions, and personal exploration.

3. Whether you have a strong faith or are still seeking, remember that a loving and compassionate God cares for all living beings, including animals.

4. If you feel comfortable, share your thoughts and questions about faith with others who may have similar experiences or insights. Engaging in open and honest conversations can be enlightening.

5. Hold onto the hope that the best is yet to come. Whether in this life or the next, love, joy, and cherished reunions await those who hold steadfast to hope and faith.

CHAPTER TWO

YOUR LOVE STORY HAD A PURPOSE, AND IT'S NOT OVER!

2.1

YOU ARE NOT ALONE

*The most beautiful people we have known are those who have
known defeat, known suffering, known struggle, known loss,
and have found their way out of the depths. These persons
have an appreciation, a sensitivity, and an understanding
of life that fills them with compassion, gentleness, and a
deep loving concern. Beautiful people do not just happen.*

ELISABETH KUBLER ROSS[3]

How can I feel so alone when most of my friends and family are trying to support me in the best way possible? How can I feel so alone in a room full of familiar faces and sympathetic hearts? How can I feel so alone when I know other pet parents have been through this devastating type of loss and seem to make it through to the other side?

These questions run through our minds while we are on our grief journey, sometimes daily. I bet you've silently asked yourself even more questions about feeling alone on this journey than the ones I mentioned above.

How could we not feel alone when our hearts feel like they are being ripped out of our chests? This pain is an almost unexplainable type of pain most of us have never experienced. Yes, it's extremely common to feel alone.

But the truth is, we are not alone.

The more we recognize our pain, sorrow, and grief as part of a bigger picture, the more we can see it for what it is: a way to deeply connect with others while our hearts heal. I believe we are here on earth to embrace life's good, bad, and ugly so we can share our experience, strength, and hope with others God places on our path. Another way to put it is that we are here to pay it forward—whether it's joyful abundance or the wisdom gleaned from sorrow.

This outlook on life comforts me, and I hope it will comfort you, too. Let me explain.

One of the best ways to connect deeply and meaningfully with others is to allow ourselves to be transparent. The definition of transparent is "allowing light to pass through so that objects behind can be distinctly seen" and "having thoughts, feelings, or motives that are easily perceived."[4]

I don't know about you, but I don't want to be transparent when I'm in pain. I want to pull the shades down in my house, watch mindless TV, and eat Cheez-Its or gummy bears. I want to hide my struggles and emotions, pretending to be okay and handling them well because I do sometimes care about what others think of me. It always feels better to be seen as capable and put-together. The alternative is to possibly be seen as messy or dysfunctional—neither of which is flattering, right? I know I'm not perfect. I shouldn't care what others think, but I do care at times.

A vivid example of this is from back in my drinking days. I tried my hardest to be transparent but couldn't because I hid the secret under the guise of having it all together, even when I didn't. But now that I'm sober, I know that transparency is a key to healing.

Transparency is powerful, but it takes practice. In fact, it takes daily practice. If we hide behind perfectionism, pride, and performance, others cannot see all God is doing for us now or what he has done in the past.

Contrary to popular belief, transparency is far from showing weakness; it's a demonstration of God's power to change our lives because when we are transparent with others about our pain, it allows them to meet us where we are, encourage us with hope for divine healing, and comfort from their own experiences with loss.

Helping others when we are in a "funk-a-delic" (Simon and I made up this term for when we are in a bad mood, having a pity party, or feeling down in the dumps) is one of the best ways to elevate our mood while taking our mind off of ourselves.

Take time today to share your sorrow with a friend who has suffered their own loss, and then reach out to someone who is struggling and let them know they are not alone either. I encourage you to do this every day and watch how your mood changes for the better, your outlook on your particular problems dissipates, and your heart feels wholesome and connected in a new way.

Remember that grief is a natural process, and everyone experiences it differently. Finding support and connection with others can be crucial in healing and moving forward after losing your beloved pet. Being open and transparent about your feelings can lead to more meaningful relationships and a sense of belonging in a community that understands and empathizes with your journey.

Today, someone wants to see the real you!

RACHEL'S REFLECTIONS & REMINDERS

1. It's common to feel alone even when surrounded by supportive friends and family, especially when experiencing the pain of losing a beloved pet.

2. Move beyond perfectionism to be open and honest about your struggles and emotions, allowing others to see your authentic and genuine self.

3. Being transparent takes effort and daily practice, but it can lead to powerful connections and positive change in your life.

4. Reach out to others who are struggling, even when you are feeling down yourself. Supporting others can uplift your mood and shift your focus away from personal struggles.

5. Knowing that others have faced similar challenges and found ways to cope can provide comfort and hope during difficult times.

REFLECTING ON THE PRICELESS GIFT OF YOUR PET

So, my very dear friends, don't get thrown off course. Every desirable
and beneficial gift comes out of heaven. The gifts are rivers of light
cascading down from the Father of Light. There is nothing deceitful
in God, nothing two-faced, nothing fickle. He brought us to life
using the true Word, showing us off as the crown of all his creatures.

JAMES 1:16–18, MSG

To this day, I still remember the peaceful joy Winston brought Simon and me daily. As I reflect on the pure joy and unfiltered love he exuberated, I think of how God designed him for our pleasure, comfort, and fun while on earth.

Astonishingly, our Heavenly Father thought about how we would have trials, tribulations, celebrations, and successes, and He wanted us to have the purest form of love by our side. That's how I describe our beloved pets, the purest form of love we have ever experienced.

My friend, God loves you so much that He created your sweet ones, hand-delivered them to you, and even in their death, He brought them home with Him for you to see in heaven again.

We typically internally perceive that we own the gifts that are given to us. Right? Our material gifts from friends and family, our spiritual gifts from God, our pets, our homes, our cars, and even the breath in our lungs.

My mom introduced me to horses when I was four. I was in love and remember feeling more alive when I was around them. My parents were not wealthy, but they found a way to buy me my first horse when I was nine. Fast forward to when I was in my late twenties and had my dream horse, Sibille.

Sibille was a beautiful Dutch Warmblood mare imported from Holland. My mom had received a small inheritance and bought her for me. God sent her to me, and I was in heaven. She was everything I wished for and more.

Sibille was the first animal in my life that helped me understand that our animals are priceless gifts. I bet you experienced what I did, knowing what it's like to have that special animal bond that gives you a new perspective on how beautiful life can be with your beloved animal companion.

I've learned that having a deep understanding and acknowledging the divine nature of my pet's arrival in my life somehow made her departure more acceptable or understandable. In other words, God cares so much about us and greatly wants to bless us. He gives and takes away, but there is a blessing in both.

I think I know what's on your heart right about now. You tell yourself or me, "Yeah, but the best gift I have been given has died. That is unfair; it's mean, cruel, and unkind."

My beloved friend, I know you are in pain, and it's sometimes hard to understand why God does things, but perhaps it would help you to think about it this way. Our pets have an expiration date, just like we do. Think about that for a moment. We all live, and we all die. That is guaranteed. But I believe you will see your priceless gift again in heaven one day.

No matter how long or short your time was with your sweet one, your love story will never die. The hope of heaven reminds us that this time on earth— and the grief we are experiencing right now—is temporary. A new chapter to our story will begin in eternity one day! That's something to celebrate!

The more you can embrace and rehearse the fact that your pet was heaven-sent by God Himself, the more I believe you'll realize your love for and with them is not over. Instead, consider it a pause on the journey until you meet again in heaven.

My friend and veterinarian Dr. Derrick Pinney shared with me:

> "I believe that animals come into this world with the full ability to love unconditionally, and that is imparted to them from God. We as humans have to learn to love in this way, and God gives us these babies to help us on that path. That is why we must live longer, in order to rid ourselves of selfish love and turn to unconditional love."

RACHEL'S REFLECTIONS & REMINDERS

1. Reflect on the joy and unconditional love that pets bring into our lives. God designs them as a source of pleasure, comfort, and fun.

2. Acknowledge that our gifts, including our beloved pets, are blessings from God, and we don't own them. We are simply managers of their care for a time.

3. Embrace the understanding that though our pets have an expiration date, we can find comfort in believing we will be reunited with them in heaven.

4. Consider the time apart from our pets as a temporary pause until we are reunited in heaven.

5. Look forward to the joyous reunion with our beloved pets in heaven, holding onto the hope that their departure is not the end of the love story.

ACCEPTANCE IS A GIFT

Acceptance of death is part of the work that
must be done if we are to grieve fully.

ELISABETH KUBLER ROSS[5]

How often have you heard it's best to accept what is because you can't change the outcome? Sometimes, you can change an outcome if the situation allows it, but usually, our pet's health prognosis is not something we can decide.

When our beloved pets approach the end of their lives, our emotions and instincts might lead us to attempt to take charge of the situation. However, the reality is, in most instances, we are not in control. Diseases and accidents happen, and there is rarely anything we can do to change the outcome.

We don't have some magical power to keep them alive, and no amount of prayer, positive thinking, or human expertise can change God's plan for the lives of our pets. The Bible says our days are numbered (Job 14:5). He has marked out a plan for our lives and our pets' lives.

As I mentioned previously, we all have an expiration date, and there's no way around it. When it's our or our pets' time—it's simply time. The more we resist this simple but hard-to-accept truth, the more we stay stuck and unable to move into a place of acceptance, which is part of the grieving process.

Acceptance is hard to grasp, but when you do grasp it, it will come with peace and purpose. So, how do we accept what we want to deny?

Well, this is all about having an insightful perspective. It's been my experience that when we humble ourselves enough to recognize and understand that God is the one who calls the shots, then we naturally release our human tendency to think we know what's best or how events should unfold in our lives.

Sure, we are partners with Him, but ultimately, He has the final say. He is the one who created your loved one, and He is the one who knows when their expiration date is.

Whenever I start to think I know more than God, I experience the most pain and disappointment in my heart.

His ways are not our ways, and His thoughts are not our thoughts (Isaiah 55:8–9) because He is God, the Creator of the universe, so He sees everything and knows what is best for His creation. Thinking I have a say in the matter is futile.

This doesn't mean God doesn't care about what we want or think. He sure does. After all, He is a good Father and loves us unconditionally and without fault. He will never withhold His best from us. We must remember that He has the vantage point of seeing the *whole* picture of our lives, which means He knows what is best for us, even when it might not make sense or feel good.

I know that might be hard to hear, but I promise you that there is freedom with acceptance. Acceptance frees your heart from needless suffering.

We all suffer; it's the amount and frequency of it that we get to control. We cannot control the outcome of our pet's death, but we can control our reaction to it and how long we let it impact our joy.

I suggest that the next time you find yourself ruminating on the last days and moments of your pet's life in despair, you try to remember the gift of acceptance and how much freedom you have in letting yourself off the hook for being human and powerless over the things you could not control.

My beloved, what would happen if you simply accepted your sweet one's passing just as it happened? Would that make you a terrible pet parent? No. Would it change the love you both experienced? No.

Rather, it would allow you to focus on the things that matter most to you in your grief— the memories of their beautiful life and the lessons they taught that you carry with you.

I can tell you for sure that the sooner you move into acceptance, the sooner you'll stop beating yourself up over what you couldn't possibly have controlled or changed.

That's a great place to start taking good care of yourself while on this healing journey.

Acceptance is a valuable gift we can give ourselves during the grieving process. It allows us to embrace the natural course of life and let go of unnecessary suffering caused by resisting the inevitable.

By surrendering to God, acknowledging our human limitations, and accepting the reality of our pet's passing, we can find peace, purpose, and healing in our hearts.

RACHEL'S REFLECTIONS & REMINDERS

1. Accepting the reality of your pet's passing is essential, even though it can be tempting to resist this outcome.

2. Realize that, as humans, we have limitations and cannot control certain outcomes, especially in matters of life and death.

3. Acceptance brings peace and purpose, allowing us to align with the natural order of life.

4. While we cannot control the outcome, we can control how we react to it by choosing acceptance over resistance.

5. Recognize that being human means we are not all-powerful, and it's okay to let go of trying to control the uncontrollable.

YOU CAN HAVE COMFORT AND HEALING

Even though I walk through the darkest valley, I will fear no evil,
for you are with me; your rod and your staff, they comfort me.

PSALM 23:4

What does comfort mean to you? For some, it means receiving loving care from a person, place, or thing. For others, it means allowing yourself to be consoled while in pain or distress. For me, it means recognizing that the human part of us desires to feel safe and on solid ground when our world feels as though it's been torn apart.

Do you see a theme here in each response? Each involves recognizing, allowing, and receiving. We must recognize what brings us comfort, and then we must allow ourselves to receive it. Don't deny yourself the tremendous healing that comes through whatever form of comfort is meaningful and helpful to you, my friend.

While working with many individuals and families over the years, I have encountered several clients who, in such a deep place of pain, deny themselves a healthy means of comfort.

There are plenty of reasons for this, but one in particular that I want to land on is the thinking that by denying comfort, you are showing yourself and the world how much pain you are experiencing. If this is your tendency, you are not alone, but it's not the best way to navigate your grief.

Let me be frank here. Sometimes, we want to stay in our own little pity party for one. I know I do when the pain feels unbearable. Isolation feels oh so good, but only for a brief moment. The truth is we are designed for companionship, especially when we are in pain.

When our sweet ones died, our companionship went with them. However, when you are in grief, it is not the time to try to be strong and go it alone. You need others. You need the comfort they want to share with you.

In fact, providing comfort to others is a gift from God. It's a language of love from one person to another, often rooted in deep care and personal experience. When we go through something and experience the comfort of others, it's natural to then pass it on to others in similar pain.

Some people console others more naturally than others. They know exactly what to say and do to help. While others run away from pain, these people run toward the pain in an effort to help.

Some people struggle to know what to say or do, and that's okay. Look for how they offer comfort in their own way too, whether it be a check-in text via the phone, a card of condolences, or a hug without words.

If you look hard enough, most people in your life want to bring you comfort. You just have to be open to accepting it. My desire is to remind you that your pain is worth seeing, feeling, expressing, and releasing as you are on your grief and healing journey.

Before your pet passed, I think it's safe to say that they provided you with the most comfort. They knew exactly how to comfort you without even knowing they were doing it.

Just the simple wet nose pressed against your face or their paw placed on your arm while you were having a tough day was enough care to help you get past it. Or how about that big bark when someone's at the door, providing us with the best guard dog around to let the person knocking know your dog means business and not to mess with your family?

Our pets brought great comfort day in and day out. We are designed for relationships that provide a sense of security, wholeness, and well-being, whether from our pets or people. We shouldn't deny ourselves healthy means of comfort.

Notice I said "healthy" there? What we choose to comfort us in our time of need matters. It's healthy to desire comfort as long as the desire is not met with a dependency on the person, place, or thing providing us comfort.

Healthy comfort through people and everyday things—like a warm and cozy blanket, a hot bath, a cup of tea, a friend's voice on the other end of the phone, or a visit from a loved one—can be quite helpful. But, as we know, there can be unhealthy things that we can run to in times of stress, like a bag of chips, a tub of ice cream, alcohol, pain pills, etc.

Here's my ask of you: just be willing to recognize what will bring you healthy forms of comfort, and then be ready to allow yourself to receive it because you are worth it, my love.

RACHEL'S REFLECTIONS & REMINDERS

1. Comfort is essential for healing and coping with pain and distress.

2. Allow yourself to receive comfort from others, acknowledging that it is a valuable part of the healing process.

3. Don't deny yourself the healing that comes from seeking and accepting comfort in healthy ways.

4. Instead of isolating yourself, recognize the importance of companionship and the support of others during the grieving process.

5. Seek comfort in healthy ways that don't lead to unhealthy dependencies.

LOOK FOR DIVINE CONNECTIONS

Your eyes saw my unformed body; all the days ordained for me
were written in your book before one of them came to be.

PSALM 139:16

We often see life's divine connections and lessons in the rearview mirror. But as you train yourself to look for divine connections in the current moment, life becomes much more interesting, satisfying, and harmonious.

Seeing how God is in the details of your love story with your sweet one can bring about a new appreciation for how much God loves you yesterday, today, and for eternity.

When my horse Sibille was in my life, I could see how God used her to help me see that life was worth living. I was trying to find my place in this world at that time. I was in my late twenties and single after a recent breakup when I got her.

One of the ways I chose to add comfort to my life before her arrival was by doing what many young adults do—drinking wine to help me relax in the evenings. The truth is, though, I drank a few glasses of wine every night and became dependent on it to help me cope with stress.

In our society, alcohol is an acceptable and encouraged way to unwind, take the edge off, and temporarily forget about our problems, or so I thought.

What a lie! I felt a massive disconnect between how God wanted me to live and what society said about drinking alcohol.

Many people can drink socially and never become dependent on alcohol. I desperately wanted my drinking to look like that, but it did not. I loved how it made me feel. I simply struggled to put the alcohol down. Alcohol was like my best friend, always there when I needed it. It was the only thing that really seemed to ease my stress, or so I thought. Finally, my life came to a point where I thought about what I was doing here and whether life was worth living.

As I reflect on those days, I can now see the divine connection of God bringing Sibille into my life to give me some new meaning and purpose in that season. I took excellent care of her even when I couldn't care for myself as well as I wanted to. I believe she saved my life.

Honestly, if she had not been in my life, I might have seriously contemplated ending my life. That's how desperate my struggle with drinking became.

Those moments and experiences can define the trajectory of our life. Look around, beloved friend. There are divine connections all around you if you will only see and embrace them.

Your sweet one coming into your life is one of the most precious and divine connections you'll ever make. The point I'm making here is when we reflect and look back, even though we might be in pain right now because our sweet one is no longer with us physically, we can see how tender, sweet, loving, honoring, and cherishing our Creator is by allowing our time with our sweet one here on earth to be so beautiful and to have such a unique relationship.

My prayer for you now is that you will take some time to see the goodness of God around you. The example I used about alcohol may be a dramatic one, but by the grace of God, I have been a sober woman of God for over a decade now.

I see God at work divinely in the good and the bad now. You can, too—if only you will look for Him.

RACHEL'S REFLECTIONS & REMINDERS

1. Train yourself to look for divine connections and lessons in your current life.

2. Recognize how much God shows his love for you through the experiences you shared with your beloved pet.

3. Reflect on past experiences and see how divine connections have influenced the trajectory of your life.

4. Acknowledge the special and unique bond you shared with your pet, seeing it as a precious divine connection.

5. Be willing to share your experiences and the lessons you've learned to encourage and inspire others.

CHAPTER THREE

THIS GRIEF THING SUCKS

3.1

THIS IS NORMAL

*Grief is arguably the hardest thing we as humans
ever experience. It can also feel like the craziest.*

ALAN D. WOLFELT[6]

One of the questions I am frequently asked is, "Is what I'm feeling normal?" I always lovingly and reassuringly answer, "Absolutely. This is normal."

Humor me for a minute while I define *this* and *normal* regarding feelings during pet loss grief. But before I share my insights on what is normal, let me first highlight what is not normal.

Self-harm, harming others, debilitating depression, suicidal ideations, thoughts of threats, and extreme isolation are not normal and need to be addressed immediately if you experience them. If you are being plagued by a desire to engage in any of these things, please contact the suicide hotline or your doctor immediately for help. You are not alone, and the world needs you.

Okay, back to what *this* and *normal* are, from my experience.

This can be defined as the emotional roller coaster of feelings before, during, and after your pet's death. It's the emotions, sleepless nights, visions of your sweet one walking around your house, thinking you hear them, not being able to put words together about how you are feeling and coping, confusion, brain fog, lack of desire to be with people, being unable to perform and concentrate at work, uncontrollable crying, anger, frustration, feeling emotionally numb, feeling physically sick, headaches, fatigue, and let's not forget about asking yourself if you can make it through this pain.

Normal can be defined as asking, "Does everyone go through the same roller coaster?" or "Is my painful reaction to their death exaggerated?" and "Is obsessing on the last moments of their death something I'm doing alone or do other people in this situation do it too?"

What you experience while grieving your sweet one is important, valid, unique, typical, natural, normal (although not pleasant), and necessary for your human experience.

Perhaps you've heard it said that we are human beings having a spiritual experience here on earth. This is so true. And yes, your experience is likely very normal, but I'm here to let you know there is hope ahead, my love!

You will get to the other side of this as a changed person—changed for the better because of your willingness to breathe and walk through the challenging moments instead of avoiding them. They won't go away through avoidance and lack of acknowledgment. In fact, it may just make them worse in the long run.

When we make a negative self-judgment (I can't be normal if I'm feeling and reacting the way I am) while self-reflecting on how we are showing up in this great time of despair (I'm too much of a mess), we close the door to growth and wisdom.

My beloved friend, please try to embrace this time in your life. Grab hold of all that God is showing you about love, loss, and life so you can pay it forward to someone else when they face the same brutal and dreadful loss. The Bible says God's Spirit comes to comfort us in our pain and grief so that we can comfort others with that same compassion (2 Cor. 1:3–4).

As you realize you are not alone and there is hope to hold onto, you can tell others grieving that they, too, are not alone and that what they are experiencing is normal and understandable.

But for today, please gently remind yourself that you are doing your best to work through a very normal and natural grief and healing journey.

RACHEL'S REFLECTIONS & REMINDERS

1. Grieving the loss of your beloved pet can be an emotional roller coaster with ups and downs. Remember, it's okay to experience a wide range of emotions during this process, as it is a natural part of grieving.

2. If you find yourself considering self-harm, harming others, extreme depression, or suicide, please seek immediate help by contacting a suicide hotline or mental health professional. Remember, there is support available for you. You are not alone.

3. Feeling isolated and overwhelmed are common parts of the grieving process, but it's essential to remember you are not alone in your experience. Many people go through similar emotions and thoughts during one of the greatest losses in life: pet loss.

4. Give yourself permission to feel the pain, confusion, and sadness in your grieving process. It's normal to have sleepless nights, visions of your pet, and difficulty expressing your emotions during this time.

5. Remember that what you are going through is a typical human experience. Grief, while challenging, is a natural response to losing your loved one. Be patient with yourself and trust that healing will come as you allow yourself to mourn.

3.2

YOU ARE NOT CRAZY!

*Nothing that grieves us can be called little: By the
eternal laws of proportion a child's loss of a doll and a
king's loss of a crown are events of the same size.*

MARK TWAIN[7]

My coaching clients often ask, "Am I crazy for feeling, thinking, or react-ing the way I am?" My answer is absolutely not. You are *not* crazy!

The thoughts that went through my mind (when Winston passed), my client's mind, and most likely your mind are, "I don't know when I will stop crying," "I don't know how I'm going to survive my sweet one's death," "Why can't I think straight?" "Will I ever be happy again?" and "Am I crazy for car-ing so much about an animal?"

My friend, you are not crazy. You are in a very natural state of mourn-ing and surviving. Right after our loss, we often feel confused, with a sense of shock and disbelief that our sweet one has left us. Truthfully, the shock of our new reality can feel like an out-of-body experience. We can't make sense of reality, and it affects everything unexpectedly.

Maybe you can relate. The sudden onset of symptoms like brain fog, extreme fatigue, confusion, depression, eating unhealthy foods in search of comfort, being unable to eat because your appetite is gone, isolation, and retreating from social events and obligations invade your life.

You may feel like you're going crazy when this long list of symptoms overcomes you, but let me assure you, it's all a natural and expected part of the grieving process.

I remember not only being in shock about our beloved boxer, Winston's, sudden and dire diagnosis but also about facing and deciding to follow his vet's recommendation to have a peaceful passing right away to end his suffering. By the way, this all happened on the same day.

I was devastated.

I just decided to have my best friend euthanized to end his suffering from his brain tumor and cancer all over his body (in which the symptoms never surfaced until a few days before his diagnosis).

And after all that agony, I had to go home and watch his brother (from another mother), Spencer, look all over the house for him. It was tragic, to say the least. My heart was broken, my mind was confused, and it felt like my little safe and happy world was suddenly shattered. It was incredibly hard to make sense of it all.

And, as I'm sure you can relate, there was the stress of normal day-to-day stuff that was piled on top of my grief and certainly couldn't be paused. There was stress and pressure from my job, and a new (very expensive and necessary) roof was being put on our house after a tumultuous hurricane season in Florida. Oh, and I work from home, so you can imagine the noise and distraction that made. It was a lot to carry.

I couldn't think straight.

I couldn't eat.

I couldn't feel.

I was lost.

Honestly, I felt a bit crazy. But the truth is, I was not crazy; I was going through what you and I and many other devoted pet parents do, facing the devastating loss of our beloved and perfect pet while dealing with the normal hard things of life.

Not only can the regular day-to-day life stressors increase the stress we feel from the death of our beloved pet, but having others' opinions of how we should handle it all can be the very thing that puts us over the edge.

People (often with good intentions) can say hurtful things while we're grieving.

For example, "Why don't you get another pet?" as if the new pet could replace the love of our life, or "He lived a good long life. Just be grateful you had so much time together!" or "At least it's just a pet and not like your child died!"

I heard some of these statements, and I bet you have, too. You can probably add some to this list.

Additionally, some people you know (even family members) tend to rank death's importance and how much, long, or even if grieving is acceptable to them in their eyes. They seem to think losing a person is more important than the devastating loss of a pet, one of the closest relationships in which you've experienced pure unconditional love, acceptance, forgiveness, and loyalty.

Here's what I want you to know, though: other people's opinions are just opinions, not facts.

We love our family and friends. We know they care for us, but sometimes they don't understand the pain we're going through because they have not been through it themselves—or even if they have, perhaps they didn't really grieve their loss the way you do.

So when good-intentioned people say words that sting your heart and make you question your sanity through this traumatic loss, remember you were the one who was blessed to encounter one of the best relationships in your life.

It's normal and natural to mourn and grieve in your unique way, so just keep walking down the path one day at a time. Your head and heart are trying to figure out what happened and how to reconcile your new reality without your sweet one. This is hard work, and not everyone around you will understand. However, I'm here to tell you that you are not alone.

I'm here, and there are people who have walked this path and are a little way beyond you, who will gladly turn back and show you the way. And whether you believe it or not, the One who created you cares for you, too. Our Heavenly Father loves us unconditionally. He is our ultimate healer, restorer, protector, and provider. He has been and will always be taking care of you—no matter how heavy it all seems.

I understand you may not feel that way right now, and that's okay. God can handle whatever you think and feel. His greatest desire is for you to come to Him authentically, honestly, broken, and just as you are because He loves you unconditionally and wants to communicate with you and mend your broken places.

God is never far away. In fact, He is with you right now, at this moment, inviting you to share with Him whatever is on your heart—the good, the bad, the ugly. All of it. He has you in the palm of His hand, loving you like no other can.

Remember, this feeling of being crazy will disappear in time. Your grieving process is your unique journey. Believe it or not, this painful season in your life is temporary, not permanent. So, although you've heard it a zillion times, a helpful phrase to remember is, "This too shall pass." With every day that passes, you will see you are surviving this painful loss. There is hope. You will get through this in time.

Here is my prayer for you today:

> *Heavenly Father, thank you for never leaving us or forsaking us. You are the ultimate healer, and we need your tender loving care and gentle healing in this moment and forever. We ask you to show us how to bring more self-care, rest, and serenity as we grieve the most precious gifts you gave us, our sweet ones. Thank you, Lord, for always being accessible and available. In Jesus' name, Amen.*

RACHEL'S REFLECTIONS & REMINDERS

1. Avoid being too hard on yourself for feeling overwhelmed or questioning your sanity. Treat yourself with kindness and self-compassion during this difficult time.

2. Recognize that people may not fully understand your pain, and their well-intentioned words may not always be comforting. Focus on knowing your grief is valid and significant.

3. Surround yourself with people who can empathize with your grief and provide support without judgment. Seek support groups or online communities to connect with others who have experienced pet loss.

4. If you find your grief overwhelming or affecting your daily life significantly, consider seeking help from a grief coach like me, a counselor, or a therapist. Professional support can provide valuable tools for coping with grief.

5. Acknowledge your strength and resilience through this challenging time. You can navigate through grief and emerge stronger on the other side. I believe in you.

.

3.3

THE DEPTH OF YOUR RELATIONSHIP WAS ON PURPOSE

Animals are footprints of God.

MARTIN LUTHER[8]

God created animals, specifically our pets, to reflect how He cares about and loves us as His children. It's been my experience—and the experience of countless clients, friends, and family members—that our pets are the purest form of unconditional love, forgiveness, loyalty, kindness, and grace.

Isn't it true? You were so close with your sweet one because they showed these things unconditionally and without hesitation.

For me personally, the unconditional and endless gifts our pets offer us are a huge reason I will always have a pet to take care of (ideally, more like three or four). It's not only part of our DNA to nurture, but it's a joy beyond measure to be loved by an animal.

As humans, just like animals, we thrive on nurturing relationships—both giving and receiving them.

My sweet boy Winston would intentionally come behind me and nudge his nose into my hand as if he were saying, "Hey, Mom, I'm here if you need me!" His presence and desire to nurture me like I was nurturing him brought me so much joy and validation. I believe God designed our pets to reflect His love, which we may never otherwise experience on this side of heaven.

The tender moments you shared with your pet, which are probably flooding your memory as you read this, are why God ordained our relationships with our pets to be so powerful and unforgettable, just like He is. His love is a perfect love, and our pets give us a small glimpse of that.

We will never forget the heart-centered, unsolicited, uncomplicated, and non-manipulative love we received and gave to our pets. The good thing is those memories will bring us comfort and remind us how wonderful our Heavenly Father is to have blessed us with their joy, comfort, and companionship while we are here on earth.

Another reason the depth of our relationship with our sweet one was on purpose is that God knew ahead of time which trials and tribulations we would face, and He didn't want us to go it alone. Our pets help us persevere and thrive instead of just surviving some of the traumas, delays, distractions, derailments, and dilemmas life throws our way.

God never promised life would be easy. He says clearly in His Word that we will have troubles and tribulations (John 10:10); however, I find it incredibly telling of God's loving character that he gives us the best relationship we could have ever imagined through a pet to be our companion for the ride.

My beloved, we are just passing through this life and on to the next. And guess what? If we say yes, one day, we can experience soul-satisfying companionships with other sweet ones God places on our journey.

I don't know about you, but I'm guessing you're a lot like me in having breathtaking anticipation that we will experience the level of unconditional love and unbridled joy that comes from pet companionship again, but it's totally okay if you don't.

Our God is mighty. He created the heavens and the earth. He made you, me, our pets, and our hearts for pets. He is working behind the scenes to provide your heart with healing, restoration, and the power to love again.

When I'm on my deathbed, I want to have peace, joy, and gratitude in my heart, knowing that I loved deeply, forgave quickly, and served whole-heartedly every person, animal, project, and responsibility that our Heavenly Father asked me to steward to the best of my ability, with every breath I took.

That is my prayer for you, too.

May God meet your pain with a new sense of calmness as you remember the God who created you loves you more than you know.

RACHEL'S REFLECTIONS & REMINDERS

1. As humans, nurturing others is part of our DNA. Embrace the nurturing aspect of your relationship with your pet and consider how it positively impacted both of your lives.

2. Recognize that God ordained our relationships with pets to be robust and unforgettable, mirroring His loving and caring nature. Embrace the love that God has for you and others, as demonstrated through your relationship with your sweet one.

3. Life on earth is temporary, and we are passing through to the next phase of our journey. Embrace the joy and companionship you experienced with your sweet one, knowing God's love extends beyond this life.

4. Believe in God's plan for healing and restoration in your heart. Trust that He is working behind the scenes to bring comfort, love, and companionship into your life when the time is right.

5. God deeply loves you, and His love extends beyond human relationships. Embrace the love you experienced with your sweet one as a reflection of God's unconditional and abundant love for you.

3.4

UNCOMPLICATED RELATIONSHIPS VERSUS HUMAN RELATIONSHIPS

His ears were often the first thing to catch my tears.

ELIZABETH BARRETT BROWNING[9]

Oh, how I love our relationships with our pets. They are more than animals that belong to us; they are family. And if you are anything like me, you value your pets just as much as you do your human companions (if not more in some cases).

Pets are uncomplicated. Even though they can't talk, they communicate all the time. In fact, I would say they are clearer communicators than even humans are! They say what they mean and mean what they say if you know what I mean. One of my favorite things about them is they are always happy to see you—even if you've only been gone for five minutes. Humans just don't have that level of appreciation for one another!

If someone leaves us alone and returns five minutes later, we say, "Back so soon?" or "Gosh, that was fast!" It's never "Oh my, how I missed you! That felt like an eternity!" But that's precisely what our pets think when we are reunited—even for a moment.

They also have a fantastic sense of intuition. It is hard to explain how they know what we feel even if we don't. They just sense the real us and the complexities of our emotions. They know our secrets, vices, inner struggles, and ugly moments and don't hold it against us. No masks, no agendas, no manipulation to get what they want—well, I take that part back. We know they know how to get us to give them what they want with their adorable little faces and those eyes!

The sweet meow, whiny, squeak, or bark informs us of how we can make their life perfect at that moment, and typically, we are more than willing to make it happen.

I often say to my clients, "It's incredible how we receive so much joy from seeing our sweet ones happy and content." Ain't that the truth?

But the joy in making them happy lies in the fact that it genuinely doesn't take much. A precious moment of touch, the effort to praise them, a walk outside, or a yummy treat is all they need to feel content.

We are so willing to give what they ask from us because it comes out of our loving hearts to make their lives the best possible. We can never repay them for all the joy, happiness, love, affection, comfort, and harmony they bring to our lives.

Never.

Truly, our relationship with our sweet one is so simple and uncomplicated.

In contrast, however, our human relationships can be very complicated. Sometimes, it seems easier to love animals than people. Wouldn't you agree? Especially these days when our world is not as it used to be. People seem much more self-centered, impatient, and mind-blowingly unkind today. Pets are none of those things, thankfully.

Our sweet ones are amazingly simple and wonderfully uncomplicated. Naturally, this is one of the reasons why you are grieving so profoundly. In fact, it might help you to make a list of what you loved about your relationship with your pet and then what you love about your human relationships. I think it would give you a greater understanding and context for why you are missing, mourning, and grieving your pet as you are.

My friend, humans are irreplaceable, but so are our pets. Both hold so much value in our lives; the love just shows up in different ways.

And that's okay.

RACHEL'S REFLECTIONS & REMINDERS

1. Our sweet ones offer acceptance and unconditional love regardless of our flaws and struggles. Consider emulating this quality in your human relationships, fostering a more compassionate and understanding environment.

2. Take a cue from your pet's straightforward communication style. Embrace open and honest conversations with your loved ones, fostering deeper connections and understanding.

3. Pets live in the present moment and relish each interaction. Strive to be more present and attentive in your human relationships, valuing the time spent together.

4. Recognize the value of human and pet relationships in your life. Embrace how they enrich your existence and honor the unique and valuable place each holds in your heart.

5. Your pet's legacy lives on through the love and care you share with others. Emulate their pure-hearted nature and bring a touch of their magic into your human relationships.

CHAPTER FOUR

TAKING CARE
OF YOUR
BROKEN HEART

ATTENDING TO PROFOUND LOSS

Those we love don't go away, they walk beside us every day.
Unseen, unheard, but always near, so loved, so missed, so very dear.

ALAN MACLEAN[10]

There is something quite beautiful about attending to your personal needs while mourning. As you may have already discovered, when your loss first happens, your mind and heart are trying to figure out what just happened. It's like an out-of-body experience. Your world changed in an instant.

The word attending means to be present or to deal with something. Attending is intentionally illuminating and shining a light on what needs to be addressed. The opposite of attending is neglecting. It is easy to neglect our needs on a day-to-day basis for several reasons, especially when we are in pain.

When I deny my need for rest, quiet time, and even fun because I'm too busy with work and life's obligations, I'm neglecting the nurturing and life-giving things God invites us to prioritize for our good. Unfortunately, it's easy to disregard and downplay the value of attending to what helps us live in harmony with ourselves and others.

During our grief and mourning, attending to your needs looks different than at any other time. The truth, as you probably already know, is that no one will put your grieving process and journey as a top priority until you do. We teach people how to treat us. Attending to our loss is not anyone's responsibility but ours. However, when we set the example that we are taking care of and attending to our mourning, grief, and sorrow while adjusting to a new normal, this shows others in our lives that we are intentionally trying to heal our hearts in a healthy and honoring way.

The bottom line is that when you attend to your grief, you are on a healthy healing journey without denial, minimization, or justification. Of course, our sweet one would want us to engage in a healthy healing journey, and it's definitely what our friends and family, along with our Creator, prefer us to do. When you neglect your spiritual, physical, mental, and emotional need to feel your pain, you often try to push through, thinking you will get to the other side. But, ultimately, your mind, body, and spirit will break down.

A better way is to move to the other side of grief through intentionality, self-respect, and self-compassion. You can start this at any time. Whether you just lost your sweet one or are already along your grief and healing journey, you can give it time, space, and priority. Honor your journey by welcoming your feelings. Yes, accept them as friends in your house. They are there to help you.

In no time, I think you will find your feelings don't have control over you, and they are fickle—meaning they come and go. Allowing them to surface so you can cry, scream into a pillow, write in your journal, or speak to a trusted friend are all ways to feel your feelings and then let them go. Because we know they will return, you can embrace a needed reprieve before they resurface. The good news is that the next time, they won't be as strong, and before you know it, your mind and heart will make the connection that your feelings are not bad; they just are. And that's normal!

You will shorten your grieving and healing journey because you attended to your profound loss. This is what I want for you, my friend. Be comfortable being uncomfortable for a shorter time instead of denying, delaying, or disrespecting the lovely soul God gave you. A person who feels profoundly, loves bountifully, and cares passionately for animals as God does is a person to emulate.

Above all, remember that healing is a process, and taking the time you need to attend to your profound loss is okay. By prioritizing self-care and embracing your emotions, you can navigate through grief and move towards a healthier and more fulfilling future.

RACHEL'S REFLECTIONS & REMINDERS

1. Remember that attending to your grief and mourning is crucial for healthy healing. Neglecting your needs during this time can be detrimental to your overall well-being.

2. By attending to your grief in a healthy and honoring way, you set an example for others. Showing you care for yourself during this time can inspire and encourage others to support you in your healing journey.

3. Honor your journey by welcoming your feelings and emotions. Allow yourself to feel them without judgment or resistance. Cry, write, talk to a friend, or find other ways to express your feelings and let them go naturally.

4. Approach your healing journey with intentionality, self-respect, and self-compassion. Be kind to yourself as you navigate through the grieving process. Understand that healing takes time and that feeling uncomfortable during this period is okay.

5. Remember that feelings come and go. Acknowledge that they are a natural part of the healing process and will subside with time. Embrace the ebb and flow of emotions without judgment.

4.2

TRANSITIONING FROM DESPAIR TO PEACE

Any natural, normal human being, when faced with any kind
of loss, will go from shock all the way through acceptance.

ELISABETH KUBLER-ROSS[11]

How much despair does a person need to go through?" my client Bill asked. Bill lost his beloved husky, Maliki, due to a disease a few days earlier. Tears streamed down his face as he looked at me with despair and anguish.

It's in tender, transparent, vulnerable, and authentic moments like this that healing can occur. When we are honest, open-minded, and willing to risk exposing our inner thoughts and feelings, support from another can be the healing balm to one's heart.

Despair can make you feel like you have lost all hope. Bill lost hope that his beloved boy Maliki would come home alive. The hope of a few more joy-filled years with Maliki was gone. And the hope of ever again having a dog like Maliki was beyond his wildest dreams. Despair can feel like your body is sinking in quicksand while your mind does not know what to do next, and there's no lifeline in sight. Peace, on the other hand, is having a level of acceptance of your new reality with little or no resistance.

Okay, before you shoot me here, let me explain.

Yes, in the beginning hours, days, and sometimes even months after your beloved has passed, it feels only natural to resist that this is your new reality. No one wants to believe this loss is real. Resistance, however, is the opposite of acceptance, and it comes with a cost. It's been my experience that when I resist something I can't control, I only prolong my suffering.

Life is unfair. But our Creator is our greatest vindicator and healer. He knows how much pain you are experiencing. He knows the weight of pain. He watched as his only son died on a crude cross to take on the sins of mankind. It was a brutal loss, but it served a purpose, and in the end, He is the victor over death and the grave. He is the one who has all control, and we need to surrender our incapacity to control death when it's our loved one's time.

When Bill was able to see that he had absolutely no control over how the disease took his boy's life, rather than wanting to blame the vet for not conducting more tests earlier in Maliki's life, Bill moved his heart's posture to one of more acceptance and peace rather than disillusion and despair.

This ultimately freed Bill from self-inflicting torment in his mind and heart because he learned to lean into the hard fact that he had a choice in how he could perceive and react to less-than-desirable situations, like the death of Maliki. The truth was Maliki passed from the disease that had taken his life. Bill knew this on a deeper level than he thought.

Bill continues to thank me to this day for encouraging him to do the hard work of examining his thoughts so he can have the benefits of having fewer resentments and misunderstandings while embracing the natural side effects of peace and understanding.

Don't get me wrong. The peace I'm speaking of is not about a fluffy feeling that everything is okay or that I must roll over in joy and submit to what has been done. The peace I'm speaking of is in the depths of your soul, knowing that you will heal, recover, and love again, and you are a changed person for the better because you are not bitter from your devastating loss.

I encourage you to choose peace over despair for the rest of your life. Make this a lesson and gift you wear as a badge of honor from your sweet one. You won't regret it.

RACHEL'S REFLECTIONS & REMINDERS

1. In times of despair, remember that healing can occur when you allow yourself to be tender, transparent, vulnerable, and authentic. Share your inner thoughts and feelings with someone you trust, as their support can be the healing balm to your heart.

2. Despair can feel like losing all hope, but peace comes from accepting your new reality with little or no resistance. While it's natural to resist the outcome initially, try to move towards acceptance, especially when you have no control over the situation.

3. Healing is a process, and giving yourself the time and space to grieve is essential. Understand that the path to peace may not be immediate, but with patience and self-compassion, you will heal, recover, and love again.

4. Consider seeking support from friends, family, a counselor, or a coach who can help you navigate through your grief and emotions. Talking to someone can provide a safe space to explore your thoughts and find greater understanding and peace.

5. Choose to grow from your devastating loss instead of becoming bitter. Allow yourself to be changed for the better through this experience, honoring the memory of your loved one by wearing the lesson of choosing peace as a badge of honor.

HONOR YOUR GRIEF, SORROW, AND HEARTACHE

Suffering is an inevitable part of life. When suffering comes
to us, let us accept it with a smile. This is one of the greatest
gifts God has given us: the courage to accept with a smile
whatever He gives, whatever He allows, whatever He takes.

MOTHER TERESA (AS CITED IN MATTHEW KELLEY, 2019)[12]

As I contemplated your reaction while reading this quote, I quickly realized I must say the hard things and encourage you to do the hard stuff, or I'm not doing what I'm called to do.

Sometimes, we want to hear the standard fluffy and feel-good sayings, quotes, and self-help jargon. However, our soul often longs for the truth, a new perspective to contemplate, and the unordinary.

This grief and healing journey you're on is not one for the faint-hearted. It takes tremendous courage, perseverance, and resilience to withstand the tsunami of feelings, the constant second-guessing of what just happened, and the endless thoughts of, "How will I survive this?"

I admire Mother Teresa's willingness to encourage others to see suffering in a new light. The suffering we endure means we are in the game of life. We didn't sit on the sidelines wondering what it would be like to love so deeply and experience joy so profoundly. We said yes to inviting our sweet one into our life, knowing in the back of our hearts that this day would come. And yet, we would do it all over again.

Honoring your grief, sorrow, and heartache is simply accepting the human experience of life. We are spiritual beings having a human experience on earth until we are in heaven with our Creator for eternity.

Accepting the suffering means letting go of the expectation that suffering is limited to bad people. Let's turn our suffering into an opportunity not to judge it. There is true freedom in surrendering to what is, honoring what you are going through, and turning it into a beautiful act of kindness to yourself.

Freedom means not being preoccupied with, obsessing over, or allowing someone, something, or some action to have a hold on me. Surrender means letting go of and releasing any hidden or obvious expectation that I have control over a person, situation, or action. Honor means respecting and holding a high standard for a person, place, thing, idea, feeling, etc.

Today is the day you can be free from the constant heaviness of suffering. I encourage you to surrender your past thoughts, feelings, and reactions to what you believe suffering should be, feel, and look like, and instead courageously embrace this new perspective of accepting your suffering from pet loss with a smile, knowing there is freedom in honoring where you have been, what you are going through, and the person you are becoming, because you loved so well.

Crying is honoring. You can cry, scream into your pillow, release your feelings, and have a smile on the other side. Trust me. I have done it, and I continue to do it to this very day because I will never go back to the way I used to hold on to suffering.

Mother Teresa was so right in speaking the truth that she did. It's a choice, and the choice is yours, my love. I'm cheering you on!

RACHEL'S REFLECTIONS & REMINDERS

1. Find freedom in surrendering to the reality of your suffering. Let go of the idea that you can control every aspect of your pain or grief. Allow yourself to release preoccupations and expectations, freeing yourself from the hold that suffering might have on you.

2. Honor your feelings and emotions by allowing yourself to cry, express your grief, and release your pent-up emotions. It's a healthy and essential part of the healing process, and it doesn't diminish the strength or courage you possess.

3. Consider embracing a new perspective on suffering and grief. Shift from viewing suffering as something to endure silently to an opportunity for growth, resilience, and learning to love deeply despite the pain.

4. Be kind and gentle with yourself during this difficult time. Allow yourself to feel what you feel without judgment. Show yourself the same compassion and understanding you would offer to a dear friend in a similar situation.

5. Embrace the healing journey and the person you are becoming through this process. Recognize that, though it may be challenging, it also offers opportunities for growth, strength, and a deeper understanding of yourself and life's complexities.

4.4

RELEASE UNHEALTHY THOUGHTS

We take captive every thought to make it obedient to Christ.

2 CORINTHIANS 10:5

Today is a new day. You woke up with a continuous heartbeat, seamless breaths in your lungs, and a fresh start. Yes, a fresh start.

Each day, we are given the same twenty-four hours as everyone else. God did that intentionally, so we all are on an even playing ground.

In our twenty-four hours, we have many choices. We can choose what we believe, what we think, what we feel, how we respond, what we allow to make us bitter, what we allow to make us better, what rubs off on us, what we contribute to others, and so on.

Remember how I previously shared that a good question to ask ourselves is, "Is this thought helpful or harmful?" Our thoughts lead to words, and our words lead to actions. Examining our thoughts to see the value they hold and the control they display can be an eye-opening experience. Let me be frank here. We can cause ourselves needless suffering with unhealthy thoughts, especially when we are hurt, angry, and downright emotionally overwhelmed.

My clients have me on speed dial. It's an honor to serve them this way, letting them know I'm only a phone call away for support.

Yolanda called me one night right before I went to sleep. She had traumatically lost her sweet cat, Samantha, two weeks prior and was having a hard time. Samantha had been in her life for more than seventeen years. Yolanda looked up to and had high esteem for Samantha's vets and care team throughout her life, but she had acquired a different view of Samantha's vet on the tragic day of her passing.

Yolanda was sure something happened at the vet's office to cause Samantha's death. Samantha was in the vet's office for some blood work that day, and when Yolanda went to pick her up, she could tell something was wrong with her. She asked if anything unusual had happened, and everyone said, "No, just the routine blood work." Later that evening, she found Samantha dead on the bathroom floor.

Yolanda's heart was shattered. She was confused and upset and didn't know what to do. She tried to make sense of the situation, but no sense could be made. She returned to her thoughts that something concerning had happened at the vet's office earlier that day.

We discussed the possibilities contributing to her death when Yolanda and I spoke. But most importantly, she asked the vet for her thoughts, and the vet gave her opinions. However, Yolanda was unable to accept her opinions at that moment.

Through a few conversations with Yolanda, she realized that she was holding on to thoughts that Samantha's vet had done something wrong when it was essential to remember they did everything they could for her sweet girl to keep her healthy for seventeen years.

She also realized she was causing her heart more turmoil and suffering by not trusting her vet's actions, opinions, and reassurance that nothing unusual happened the day Samantha was with them. She made heartfelt amends to her vet and the care team, sharing that she felt terrible about how she reacted. Her vet and care team let her know they completely understood how she jumped to conclusions and that many pet parents are like her—in shock right after discovering their sweet one passing.

The story ends with Yolanda becoming more aware of how, under stress and shock, sometimes we might play untrue stories in our minds as we grasp for understanding. She now sees how releasing unhealthy thoughts before they fester and become something they are not will be helpful in the future in all aspects of life.

Beloved friend, I encourage you to be willing to examine your thoughts as you navigate through your grief and healing journey. It's very natural to ruminate on negative thoughts, but this is just stinkin' thinkin'.

It doesn't do anything to serve your peace of mind or help you move forward—especially when these thoughts can't be reconciled with facts. Try to capture your thoughts and reframe them around what you do know and what you can control so you don't spend unnecessary time thinking about the wrong things. This practice will bring peace to your heart and mind while keeping you on solid ground.

Remember, releasing unhealthy thoughts is a gradual process, and taking small steps toward cultivating a more positive and compassionate mindset is okay. By examining your thoughts and letting go of those that no longer serve you, you can create space for healing and growth during your grief journey.

RACHEL'S REFLECTIONS & REMINDERS

1. Separate facts from emotions in your thought process. Emotions can cloud our judgment, and it's important to distinguish between what we know to be true and what we feel to be true.

2. Talk to trusted friends, family members, or professionals about your thoughts and feelings. Different viewpoints provide a more balanced perspective.

3. If you have concerns or doubts about a situation, talk openly with the people involved to seek clarification and understanding. Misunderstandings can often be resolved through communication.

4. Release feelings of guilt or blame that may be causing you distress. Understand that nobody is perfect; sometimes, we make mistakes in our thoughts or actions.

5. If you find it challenging to release unhealthy thoughts on your own, consider seeking support from a therapist, counselor, or coach who can guide you.

CHAPTER FIVE

TAKING CARE OF YOUR BODY EVEN IN DEEP SORROW

YOU WON'T JUST 'GET OVER IT'

I lied and said I was busy. I was busy; but not in the way most people understand. I was busy taking deeper breaths. I was busy silencing irrational thoughts. I was busy calming a racing heart. I was busy telling myself I am okay. Sometimes, this is my busy—and I will not apologize for it.

BRITTIN OAKMAN[13]

My client Sara shared with me that her health was in second place while her cat, Melody, was in the hospital after being hit by a car. Her priority was to be available whenever she could, no matter the time of the day or night, to see her sweet girl while she was recovering from her horrific injuries. Melody could die, and knowing this did not leave room for thoughts about self-care during this crisis. Sara did not want to eat, sleep, or be distracted in any way, and understandably so. She was on edge.

I bet you can identify with this. If you were in a position where you had a few hours, days, or weeks with your sweet one before they passed, it's understandable that you naturally thought more about your sweet one than your next meal or if you had enough sleep the night before. It's easy to neglect your own well-being for your pet's sake. However, when we harbor this kind of thinking, our grief and mourning deplete our bodies' physical reserves.

The brain fog, confusion, extreme fatigue, headaches, body aches, knots in your stomach, anger, frustration, and shock that many of us experience before and after the death of our precious loves are part of the process of enduring such a devastating loss. So, while these things are natural byproducts of grief, we must recognize that once our beloved pets have died and gone to heaven for our Lord to take care of them until we see them again, it's now our responsibility to take good care of our bodies—even in deep sorrow.

This doesn't mean it won't be agonizing to do, though. I can only imagine you have cried your eyes out, feeling as if the tears will never stop. And if we're honest, every tear that fell from our eyes had meaning, memories, and mourning in the middle of them.

One of my mentors, Colleen Ellis, taught me how her mentor, Alan D. Wolfelt, Ph.D., explains the difference between grief and mourning in his outstanding book *When Your Pet Dies: A Guide to Mourning, Remembering, and Healing*: "*Grief* is the constellation of internal thoughts and feelings we have when someone we love dies. In other words, grief is the internal meaning given to the experience of loss." He goes on to say, "*Mourning* is the outward expression of grief."[14]

Wow, he's right! It makes perfect sense. He says, "Over time and with the support of others, to mourn is to heal.... We've said that grief is what you feel on the inside and that mourning is the expression of grief on the outside. Mourning is 'grief gone public.'"

I have found that the more we release our tears, the more we move through our grief to our healing journey. Now, don't get me wrong when I say "moving through grief" or make any reference to "moving forward," I do not mean getting over it because we never get over it, but we learn to get through our grief to the other side.

It's been my experience many times that with good support, eventually, the pain, grief, despair, anger, resentment, heartbreak, and sadness will not sting as much when we make healthy decisions that impact our grief and healing journey. And my beloved friend, this is what I desire for you.

Remember that grief is a unique and individual experience, and there is no right or wrong way to grieve. Taking care of yourself and honoring your emotions is essential to healing. Allowing yourself to mourn and express your grief creates space for healing and transformation in your journey toward acceptance, hope, and peace.

RACHEL'S REFLECTIONS & REMINDERS

1. Understand that taking care of yourself is not selfish but a necessary part of the healing process. Grief can be physically and emotionally exhausting, and self-care is crucial for your well-being.

2. Give yourself permission to express your emotions fully. Suppressing grief can lead to long-term consequences on your physical health.

3. Understand the difference between grief (internal thoughts and feelings) and mourning (outward expression of grief). Find healthy ways to mourn and release your emotions.

4. Even during intense grief, prioritize your basic needs, like eating, sleeping, and staying hydrated. Nourishing your body is essential for coping with grief.

5. Be mindful of your limits and set boundaries with others when needed. It's okay to say no to additional responsibilities during this healing time.

DON'T NEGLECT YOURSELF

*Self-care and grief never seem to go hand-in-hand, but the
reality is that without taking care of yourself and always
taking care of others, successful grieving is nearly impossible.*

ALEJANDRA VASQUEZ[15]

E ven before we faced this dreaded outcome with our pet, we may have
lacked a sense of wholeness, physical and spiritual health, and well-being.
I encourage you to look into your heart and honestly assess your health even
before your sweet one passed.

If your health was exactly where you wanted it, you can skip this topic
and imagine me giving you a high five!

But if you are like me, the state of my health—which wasn't where I
wanted it to be before Winston got sick—continued to decrease after he died.
I worked a high-pressure job, had some financial stress, and felt burned out
on life, work, and ministry. I fully acknowledge that it was no one's fault but
my own, and I take full responsibility for not honoring my mind, body, and
soul by putting my health on my top priority list.

I thought, *I'm in my early 40's; I'll be fine. God is good to me, and He won't
let anything bad happen to me because I'm doing good work and serving others.*
Boy, was I wrong. That's simply not how God works.

Now, don't get me wrong. God is a good Father who cares for us and
wants the best for us, but we live in a fallen world where we cannot avoid

the fallout of our fallen world. So, if we let our health slip, there will be natural, negative consequences.

Of course, He can heal us, and He definitely uses difficult situations, like grief, to get our attention. And He was certainly getting mine. I had a lot of work to do to rebuild my well-being on top of the effects the grief had on my body and mind.

How about you?

I encourage you to take an honest assessment of where your health was before your pet's illness. You might find that you had work to do, and your grief only compounded and deepened your lack of physical vitality.

Now that your sweet one has passed and you are somewhere on the spectrum of grieving and healing, it's a great time to take baby steps to intentionally nurture your health back to what you know it can be. This is my heart's desire for you.

Perhaps you need to get yourself to a doctor for your annual exam and some bloodwork to get a baseline. You may need to ensure you are nourishing your body each day so you have the energy to get out of bed and be productive.

You might need to raid your cabinets and decide you won't keep low-nutrition foods in your home. Perhaps you could benefit from some stretching or a daily walk. Maybe you can add one good social interaction into your day to feel less alone and more accountable to engage with life again.

Whatever it is or whatever those things are, I suggest you take one day at a time and invite the support of a friend or loved one who can stand with you in your effort to get healthy again.

Remember that nurturing your health during and after your pet's illness or passing is beneficial for your well-being and a way to honor the memory of your beloved companion. Taking care of yourself allows you to heal, find the strength to face the challenges of grief, and move toward a place of acceptance and healing. I'm cheering you on!

RACHEL'S REFLECTIONS & REMINDERS

1. Acknowledge any neglect of your health before your pet's illness or passing. It's okay to recognize areas where you can improve and take responsibility for making positive changes.

2. Understand that caring for yourself is essential for navigating through grief and healing. Make self-care a priority, including proper nutrition, rest, and relaxation.

3. Give yourself grace and set realistic expectations for your health journey. Healing takes time, and taking baby steps toward improving your well-being is okay.

4. Consider consulting with a healthcare professional to assess your current health status and get personalized advice on improving your physical and emotional well-being.

5. Be patient and compassionate with yourself as you work towards improving your health. Avoid self-criticism and celebrate every step of progress. Every small positive change contributes to your overall well-being.

BE GENTLE WITH YOUR BODY

*The Lord will guide you always; he will satisfy your needs in a
sun-scorched land and will strengthen your frame. You will be
like a well-watered garden, like a spring whose waters never fail.*

ISAIAH 58:11

I t might not feel like it in the midst of grief, but God does want us to be healthy, strong, and full of life to help sustain us through the ups and downs—regardless of what season of life we are in.

I understand you may have questions about the truth of this when He could have chosen to spare our sweet one, and if you haven't heard this before, let me be the first to say your confusion and your questions for God are okay. More than okay, actually. Having questions and being curious is very important in helping change our lives' trajectory from grieving loss to cherishing memories.

I do not know the answer to why God allows pain and disease. Trust me, though, when I see Him in heaven, you better believe this is one of the (many) questions I will ask Him.

So, while I don't have the answers right now, I choose to trust Him and His will. I know for certain that if we chew on this question without considering God's character and His promises, it can be a stumbling block in the way of a vibrant and healthy faith.

Early on in my first days of following Christ, I contemplated why God allows pain and disease and why bad things happen to good people. In my search for peace about following a God who doesn't seem to want just to fix all the bad things, I leaned into the wisdom of a lot of wise people, studied the Bible, and made peace with who God is—even if I don't always understand *why* He is the way He is.

Now, hold on! Don't throw this book out just yet!

I know you may think that's a cop-out or naïve of me, but I think if you do a similar study, you will find that the answers of why bad things happen and why God allows it really are issues for God.

And sometimes His reasons are concealed while we are on earth. That's just the way it is.

There is God's business, like tornadoes, hurricanes, and things like that. Then, there is my business, as in my decisions, like what I want to do with my life, what I eat, who I share my time with, and who I learn from. And then there is other people's business, like what they do with their lives, how they dress, what they say and think, and how they behave.

What isn't directly my business is actually *none* of my business. I've found a lot of peace in embracing this line of thinking. And when everything shakes out, I can point to God's faithfulness in many examples throughout my life.

He always shows up—even if it doesn't look how I'd like it to.

The Creator loves you, too. He cares so deeply for us that He faithfully and consistently guides us to become the best version of ourselves—if we allow Him to. He wants us to make wise decisions in every area of our lives so we can enjoy this journey.

When we make unwise decisions, we have to face natural consequences. For example, if we eat only highly processed foods without nutrients, our bodies will put on weight, and we won't feel our best physically, mentally, spiritually, or relationally. And on the flip side, when we make healthy eating decisions, we feel better. Our lives operate more smoothly as our bodies have abundant energy, our beautiful minds have mental clarity, and we feel better about ourselves.

I know you've sat through enough health classes in school and heard enough lectures about food from your doctors to last a lifetime.

My point is God wants the best for us, and when we choose unwise thoughts, words, food, decisions, and actions, He will try to get our attention. Sometimes, it will be a gentle whisper and other times, He will use what feels like a ginormous log strategically thrown on our path to trip us up and get our attention. It's as if He's shouting, "Hey, you are going down the wrong road. Change direction before it's too late!"

Back to when Winston died. I was trudging through the motions of life while not taking time to exercise, consuming way too many Coke Zeros for a caffeine fix, and eating way too many fatty, salty, and sugary foods—you know, the yummy kind.

In the back of my mind, I knew this was not the best I could do, but it was easier, and it felt good—until it didn't. I was pushing through, thinking I could handle it all as I put my health and well-being on the back burner to keep up with the pressure and demands of work and life in general. That was a big mistake on my part.

I ended up sick and tired of being sick and tired. I won't go into the whole story, but you get my point here. It's not worth it to take shortcuts on our health and well-being. If we aren't managing it when we aren't actively grieving a significant loss, it will only be worse when we are. Trust me.

Disease grows and spreads, and when there is disease in our mind, body, and soul, there is a *dis-ease* going on. It's destructive and pulls us down from being our best selves.

You, my beloved friend, can create an opportunity from this time of grief, pain, and despair and turn it into an impactful and positive change in your life. The stressful situations, overwhelming schedules, and trauma you are going through present the perfect time to put your health and well-being back into a higher priority as you navigate the loss of your sweet one.

I know it feels hard and requires so much energy to do the best things for yourself, but think of the payoff and take this time to put your health front and center. You'll feel a lot better; I promise you that.

Take a moment and ask yourself what it would feel like to look back at this moment in your life and be able to thank God and your sweet one for knowing you required some good old rest, repair, and replenishment.

You can use this time as a catalyst and become an advocate for your well-being. You are the only one who can take care of you. The choice is yours, and I know you will entertain and implement the wisest choice for you, your family, and your legacy.

RACHEL'S REMINDERS & SUGGESTIONS

1. Understand that your physical, mental, and emotional well-being is essential for navigating through grief and life's challenges.

2. Be open to asking questions and learning about ways to improve your health and lifestyle.

3. Avoid self-criticism and be kind and compassionate with yourself as you work on making positive changes.

4. Pay attention to your body's signals and needs. Rest when necessary and nourish yourself with wholesome food.

5. See grief as an opportunity to prioritize your health and make impactful changes in your life.

BE HONEST WITH YOURSELF ABOUT UNHEALTHY HABITS

Without courage, we cannot practice any other virtue with consistency. We can't be kind, true, merciful, generous, or honest.

MAYA ANGELOU[16]

As you can imagine, I work with countless families from whom I have the honor and privilege of hearing their deepest secrets about how they have coped with stress, pain, and loss. It isn't always pretty. And if we are all honest, none of us do things perfectly on this healing journey through grief.

We tend to reach for the oh-so-delicious container of ice cream in the freezer or that tucked-away bag of chips in the kitchen pantry as we have tears in our eyes, thinking about how our world will never be the same again. (In full disclosure, my favorite go-tos are Cheez-Its or gummy bears.)

Maybe food is not what brings you the comfort you're searching for. Maybe, like the me of the past, you turn to alcohol. My vice was wine, to be specific. I loved it because it took the edge off and quieted my mind's continuous replay of the source of my pain, like regrets and reality.

Maybe it's not alcohol that numbs you out. Perhaps you are a workaholic, so you dive into project after project, trying to distract yourself from feeling your pain. Or maybe you don't want to be productive, so you zone out on mindless TV shows to take your mind off things.

Whatever it is for you—if you are truthful with yourself, you know what you use to cope with pain—you need to recognize it for what it is: an attempt to escape from your emotions, feelings, thoughts, and reality.

By God's grace, I kicked alcohol to the curb and retired from drinking over a decade ago. Quitting drinking was the best decision of my life behind accepting Jesus into my heart and every aspect of my life. I still sometimes struggle with reaching for comfort food in stressful seasons of life. I'm happy to acknowledge that I am a work in progress for sure.

In fact, one of my mottos for moving through grief is "Progress, Not Perfection." We are all a work in progress.

I don't do things perfectly. I make plenty of mistakes. Believe me, I resist and make excuses for why healthy changes won't work or are for another time with the best of them. Sound familiar? It should be because we are all guilty of this at some time or another.

But here's the thing I want you to think about right now: Stress, pain, trauma, and loss are not an excuse to overlook the effects of self-sabotaging thoughts and unhealthy habits. These are the exact times we need to be gentle with ourselves, be kind to ourselves, and intentionally take care of ourselves with choices that build us up, not blow us up.

Choices that build us up look different for everyone. As I mentioned, this grief and healing journey you are embarking on takes courage, inner strength, dignity, and grit simultaneously. Your journey is a unique one. No two people go on this journey in the same way or experience identical thoughts, emotions, and feelings and interpret them the same.

Because of this, each of us will have to weed out the things that can blow up our potential or set us back in health and healing. And we must embrace the things that will build us up to wholeness again. This is a cognitive decision we have to make, and it's a crucial one.

Again, I'm not suggesting perfection is the ideal or even reasonable to strive for. We have to recognize that we won't always get this right, so being gentle with yourself is paramount during this heartbreaking time you are going through. Give yourself the benefit of the doubt, knowing you are doing your best with what's in front of you. And give yourself grace when you are not being the best version of yourself.

Be less judgmental of yourself, especially when you are down. Take it one day at a time and get back up each day if you fell the day before.

I invite you to take a small step in allowing rest into your spirit and to know this situation is not permanent; it's only temporary, and you will get through this. Remember that breaking unhealthy habits is a journey, and it's okay to encounter obstacles along the way. The key is to be persistent, compassionate with yourself, and committed to nurturing healthier habits that support your well-being and healing journey. With time and effort, you can create positive changes that will impact your life and overall happiness.

RACHEL'S REFLECTIONS & REMINDERS

1. Acknowledge and be honest about any unhealthy habits you may have developed as coping mechanisms during times of stress, pain, or loss. I mean, really honest.

2. Embrace the idea of progress over perfection and celebrate each small step towards healthier habits.

3. Discover and adopt healthier coping mechanisms that support your well-being, such as exercise, meditation, journaling, or spending time in nature.

4. Embrace imperfection and learn from setbacks. Remember that growth comes from learning, adapting, and persevering.

5. If your unhealthy habits are deeply ingrained and challenging to address, consider seeking support from a therapist or counselor. This may be one of the best decisions you will ever make.

5.5

INTENTIONAL SELF-CARE

You can be pitiful, or you can be powerful, but you can't be both.

JOYCE MEYER[17]

Intentionally taking care of ourselves can look like making a smoothie for good nutrition to replenish our depleted minds and bodies, taking a hot bubble bath and reflecting on what you're thankful for, or going for a walk in nature and talking to God. You can allow yourself to take a restful and replenishing nap without setting a specific time to wake up or watch a good movie while snuggled up on your couch with a bowl of popcorn. Why not enjoy a cup of your favorite tea or flavored water on your porch, or make space in your day to spend in-person quality time with a close friend, or for some of us, simply get out of bed and into the shower, then get back into bed?

I know you just read through that list and envisioned your pet doing many of those things with you. "I can't enjoy that and not think about how much I miss my sweet one. It hurts so much. They were here with me just yesterday and will never be here again. I can't bear to be in this place without them."

I understand. I really do. But maybe you are screaming at me through this book, saying, "Yeah, right, Rachel! If it were that simple, I would not need this book!" Yep, you are right, my love.

We need each other to remind us of what we can do when we can't remember what to do or how to do it. So, let me stop here for a moment and thank you for letting me walk with you.

I get you. I get your heart. I get your frustration, limitations, and contemplations because I've personally been right where you are, and I work with people all over the world, helping to support them with what you are dealing with inside your mind, heart, body, emotions, home, life, and soul.

I want the best for you, so let me say that you can't get past this; you can only go through it. You get to choose who you invite on the journey, so thank you for letting me join you. My beloved, I can have faith for you when you don't have it for yourself. I can believe that one day, you will be there for those who come behind you on this daunting grief and healing journey.

This, too, shall pass, and when it does, let's look back and be proud of who we are and what we are becoming because we loved well and were deeply loved by our sweet one. If I could encourage you today, I would ask you to go back and review that list at the beginning of this entry to see if there is one thing you *can* do to take care of your body and soul today.

Would you do that? I think you'll find it puts you a step further down the path of healing. Remember that healing from losing a beloved pet is a personal journey; there is no "right" way to grieve. Be open to exploring what works best for you and allow yourself to take the necessary steps to move forward while honoring the memory of your sweet one.

RACHEL'S REFLECTIONS & REMINDERS

1. Please, please, give yourself permission to kick perfectionism to the curb. Perfectionism is overrated. It debilitates our true selves and stifles our growth, transformation, and well-being. You deserve to find your unique way through this messy and uncharted journey through your grief and healing.

2. HALT: Hungry, Angry, Lonely, Tired. When you are hungry, angry, lonely, or tired, it is not the wisest time to have deep conversations or make decisions. Simply ask yourself when you become agitated, irritated, annoyed, grumpy pants, etc., if you need to HALT. Identify what needs attending to: Am I Hungry? Eat something nutritious. Am I Angry? Find a safe outlet to express feelings. Am I Lonely? Call a friend. Am I Tired? Rest or nap

3. Allow yourself to take restful breaks or naps when needed without pressure to follow a rigid schedule.

4. Allow yourself the space and time you need to grieve without feeling pressured to "move on" before you're ready.

5. Embrace hope for the future and believe in your ability to heal and create a meaningful life, even in the midst of grief.

CHAPTER SIX

NAVIGATING RELATIONSHIPS WHILE GRIEVING

YOU WERE CREATED FOR RELATIONSHIPS

Grief is not a disorder, a disease, or a sign of weakness. It is an emotional, physical, and spiritual necessity, the price you pay for love. The only cure for grief is to grieve.

EARL A. GROLLMAN[18]

I've heard it said that grief is the price we pay for love. I've also heard it said that the depth of your relationship determines the depth of your grief.

What are your thoughts when you hear these two statements? Do you find them to be true for you? Are they relevant in your life? Or do you disagree with them and find other ways to describe why your grief hurts so badly?

The truth is we were created for relationships, so our lives are centered around them. Think about that for a moment. Even if you are the most introverted person you know, you still have relationships in your life. You have some type of relationship with your coworkers or clients, your family and friends, and those with whom you share hobbies.

We all have relationships. The difference is in their depth and level of comfort. Each is in a different stage, such as developing, maintaining, or separating in one form or another. No matter their current status, God designed us to be in these relationships. We get to be in a relationship with Him and those He places in our lives.

I can see the correlation between the amount of sorrow, grief, pain, and mourning I experience and the depth of the relationship that has ended, whether it is a human or animal. When Winston passed, I was in deep sorrow over his death. He was part of our family and with us for eight years. He was basically with us everywhere we went. I bet you can relate. Our sweet ones are like velcro and follow us around constantly, don't they? Even when you go to the bathroom, they come along!

When my clients ask why this pain and grief feels so debilitating, I remind them that we were designed for relationships and, more than likely, this was one of the most significant relationships of their lives. Perhaps you can relate?

They often share with me that they are grieving more deeply after losing their sweet one than when their parents or another significant person in their life passed. My friend, if you also feel this way, it's more common than you think, and there is absolutely nothing to be ashamed about.

If I were to take out my calculator and calculate the number of days, months, and years you were with your sweet one, it would be a significant amount of time. For example, Simon and I had Winston in our lives for eight years. Multiply eight times 365 days a year, which is 2,920 days, 96 months, or 8 years we were together.

Now imagine all that time spent together, with him sleeping in our bed, going to breakfast with us, watching movies together, going to the beach, etc. We were inseparable (whenever possible) for all that time.

I'm going out on a limb here by saying I doubt you were with your parents or someone else as many hours in as many days, months, and years as you were with your pet. If you were, you know exactly how much time together factors in the depth of grief you naturally experience.

Please don't get me wrong here. I am not dismissing or downplaying our relationships with our parents and significant others. With all sincerity, I'm simply illustrating to you that the depth of your relationship with your sweet one was, in fact, different in many ways, which can illuminate how significant the grief you are experiencing. And it may very well be different from the grief you experienced when you lost a family member or friend in the past.

Yes, this grief thing sucks, my friend!

No matter how significantly you feel this loss versus others, it's still grief, and it's just terrible. But you are not alone in feeling the way you do.

One of the most important things to remember is God will never forget how deep your relationship with your loved one was. Part of your grieving process can be incorporating self-compassion with the realization that, like many, you loved deeply and are grieving deeply because you said yes to God's love through your sweet one.

You are beautiful for accepting this relationship into your life, being a good steward in taking such excellent care of them, and providing them everything they needed to thrive here on earth.

It's okay to grieve now.

Remember that grieving is a natural and necessary process, and taking the time to heal is okay. Embrace the love and relationships that have shaped your life, and honor the memories of those who have left a lasting impact.

You are not alone on this journey; resources and support are available to help you through it. Be kind to yourself. Give yourself room to reflect on one of the most extraordinary relationships God gave you with your sweet one's unconditional love, loyalty, forgiveness, kindness, and goodness, with memories for a lifetime.

Your purpose now is not to be bitter that this relationship is gone but to become a better person because of it. Show the world who you have become because your sweet one loved you so well. Have peace in your heart, knowing it was all worth it, and you would do it again if asked.

RACHEL'S REFLECTIONS & REMINDERS

1. Think about the various relationships in your life, not just with your pet but also with people, possessions, and experiences. Relationships come in different forms and stages, from developing to maintaining and sometimes separating. Recognize the impact each relationship has had on you. Every relationship that we have had has good in it. Seek the goodness and allow it to fill your heart, mind, and soul.

2. As a human being, you were designed for relationships. Your life revolves around them, and they provide meaning and purpose. Cherish your connections with others, including your loved ones, friends, and even the technology and services you use daily.

3. Understand that grieving deeply for losing a beloved pet doesn't diminish the significance of other relationships you've had. It simply reflects the unique bond you shared with them. Be kind to yourself and show self-compassion during this grieving process.

4. Remember that you are not alone in your grief. Many others have experienced similar feelings, and there are support groups or online communities where you can connect with people who understand what you're going through.

5. Grief can be a transformative experience. Allow yourself to grow and learn from it, cherishing the lessons and memories that your loved one has left behind.

BUILD YOUR BOARD OF DIRECTORS

Plans fail for lack of counsel, but with many advisers they succeed.

PROVERBS 15:22

One of my clients struggled to move forward with his life after the death of his dog, Penelope. During our conversation, it became clear to me that he had not let people into his inner circle, and the more we talked, the more he began to realize this had become an inhibitor to his healing. It's easy to slip into isolation and alienation when we are grieving.

As you will read in the next entry, sometimes it's necessary to remove certain people from your life—or at least put relationships on pause while you are healing. But we also have a golden opportunity to build what I call a "board of directors" to support the vision and mission of our new reality.

I can see your head tilting right now because you've probably never considered this concept before, so let me tell you the secret sauce to working through grief.

You need a healthy support system when you are going through a devastating loss like this. Knowing people who have your back, can see a healthy vision for your future, and have your best interest at heart is invaluable.

These people inspire you to be the best version of yourself, and you trust them to speak truth and care into your life sensitively but honestly. You must have people to trust, lean on, and rely on now more than ever.

Most of us have friends, family members, health professionals, business professionals, and spiritual advisors in our lives. Intentionally selecting a few to help you navigate this new season of grief and new beginnings without your sweet one will help you move through your healing journey much more smoothly than if you were to try to do this alone.

We tend to initiate engagement with people in the same stage of life as us or who have been through what we are going through, so why wouldn't we do the same when we are grieving?

For example, you may currently have people in your inner circle who are more business-savvy or marriage-minded or who have kids the same age as yours. How would it feel if you had a few people by your side or on speed dial to help you make wise decisions in this season of your life? People who are emotionally available, wise, and who have experienced grief and loss?

One of my favorite and frequent prayers is, "God, please open doors that you want to open and close doors that need to be closed with opportunities, people, and possessions." Allow God the space to do this work in your life if it's the best next thing to do.

You don't have to tell this person you are calling them a "board member" if you don't want to. You can simply ask them if you can lean on them for support in this season of your life. This serves two purposes: it allows you to know whether that person can be there for you, and it gives them the courtesy of knowing their care is desired and the option to decline if they are going through something themselves or are simply engaged in a really busy season.

It also helps to clarify what kind of support you need and what it will look like so you both have clear expectations of each other. For example, you might say, "Mary, would you be open to having me call you when I'm in a dark spot while I'm grieving and mourning the death of Sam? I don't anticipate needing to call at all hours of the night; I just want to know that I can have a safe place to share what I'm feeling and know your love and wisdom will help my heart in these difficult times if you have the capacity to walk with me."

It's also helpful to let them know that you do not expect or need them to try to fix you or your feelings; it's more their willingness to listen to you and to be a caring sounding board you can rely upon.

And, of course, if they agree, ask them what parameters they need you to honor during this time if they have any scheduling considerations or family dynamics you are unaware of. It's all about communication when it comes to the invitation and expectations.

You know this, but let me pause to remind you how special you are. You are an amazing person who just needs a little TLC right now. Don't feel embarrassed by your need for this care. The people in your life will appreciate your vulnerability and gift of access. I'm sure of it.

If you do an inventory and don't know who to ask, think about who is in your life that, if the situation were reversed, you'd want to feel free to come to you. These are your people, and they will probably be more than happy to step up to your board right now.

Remember that you are not alone; people in your life genuinely care about you and want to see you thrive in this new season.

RACHEL'S REFLECTIONS & REMINDERS

1. When inviting someone to join your board, clearly communicate your needs and expectations. Let them know how they can support you and what assistance you may require.

2. Ask what they may need from you during this time, as relationships are a two-way street. Be willing to reciprocate and offer support when they need it as well.

3. Building your board of directors is about quality, not quantity. Choose a few key individuals who truly resonate with you and can offer meaningful support. These people should be willing to listen and provide comfort without trying to fix your feelings. If you feel you don't have anyone you can call on, please reach out to pet loss support groups in your local community or online. You can also go to my website for more resources: http://www.rachel-shirley.com

4. Seek God's guidance in selecting the right people for your board. Ask for wisdom and discernment in choosing individuals who will uplift and empower you during this time.

5. Your board of directors may evolve over time as your needs change and as you grow in your healing journey. Be open to new relationships and connections that can offer support and guidance.

6.3

PAUSING PEOPLE
WHILE YOU GRIEVE

*Believe me, every heart has its secret sorrows, which the world
knows not, and oftentimes we call a man cold, when he is only sad.*

HENRY WADSWORTH LONGFELLOW[19]

While I've shared my thoughts on the importance of relationships and how God designed us for them, now I'm going to share with you why it's more than okay to push pause on some of them while grieving.

I once heard the quote, "Sometimes your circle decreases in size but increases in value." I believe God uses times of turmoil, tragedy, and trauma for us to pause and embrace unforeseen circumstances as reflection points in our lives. To honestly assess and evaluate what is working, what is not, who is adding value to our lives, and who is not.

Keep with me here.

If you are honest, there are probably a few people that come to mind who don't know how to support us when we need it, ask for it, or would appreciate it.

We teach people how to treat us, so it's our responsibility to ask for what we need and be specific in what that would look like so our friends and family can have a clear picture of what they can do to help us if they choose to do so.

The people I'm referring to are the ones who can be insensitive when we need their sensitivity the most.

It's the ones who say hurtful things like, "It's just a horse; It's not like your mom died. You can get another horse, but you can't get another mom, so just get another horse, and you will be fine." Or a coworker who checks in on you and asks how you are doing and, without letting you answer sincerely, promptly changes the subject back to themselves or the weather, demonstrating they were just asking to be polite instead of out of genuine concern. Or an uncle who keeps making jokes about how you are too sensitive and emotional when other family members ask how you are doing in your grief. Or how about the social-media-only friend who thinks they know you so well that they find no issue telling you precisely what to do, think, and feel in your situation.

These are the people with whom I'm asking you to reevaluate your relationship in this season of grieving.

Giving yourself and the other person room for grace, mercy, and forgiveness is the way to go, and sometimes, that means pushing the pause button on your relationship for this tender season of grief while praying for their blessings, prosperity, and well-being.

I believe our grief journey can be an opportunity to develop and exercise our boundary muscles for our protection, healing, and well-being.

We don't need any added stress to our already stressful grieving process. We need some breathing room to have people in our lives who can see us in our weakest moments, hear our deepest pain, and welcome our vulnerability for what it is—beautiful, authentic, transparent, inviting, and human.

You might not want to end the relationship with people that come to mind in the scenarios I'm relaying to you. Still, you can push the pause button on communication with them until you feel you are in a better place to talk with them or take the opportunity to teach them how they can support you during your grief and healing journey.

I love to encourage my clients to create one-liners to have on hand for when they run into situations where they may need to explain that their sweet one passed. These are your go-to words when all the other words get muddled together with the lump of pain in your throat. It's an especially helpful tool to have in your pocket for those situations that catch you off guard.

For example, "Suzy, thanks for sharing what you think will help me right now. I'm taking time to grieve, mourn, and heal right now, so I'll be in touch when I'm in a better place."

People say the darndest things sometimes. They are usually well-meaning and have great hearts, but communicating with them can feel like too much work when grieving. And when we give access to people who make it feel like too much work, we can easily take offense, and that's precisely where resentments are born and harbored.

Let's take responsibility for our healing, growth, and well-being by avoiding resentments and pushing pause on relationships or acquaintances that we can pick back up when we feel stronger and more resilient.

Let's give people the benefit of the doubt with grace, believe the best in them, and be kind to them while caring for ourselves today, tomorrow, and forever.

As I mentioned before, I'm not a therapist or a counselor. I am a faith-filled and hope-filled woman committed to compassionately sharing my experience and speaking strength and hope into your life, knowing you will take any helpful suggestions and leave the ones that are not.

That is how God works.

He often works through people who come across our path, illuminating something we have been feeling in our hearts as confirmation or saying something we have never been able to hear before until that moment and from that exact person and situation.

Remember, too, that everyone's grief journey is unique, and you have the right to decide how you navigate through it. Prioritize your well-being and healing, and surround yourself with those who genuinely support and uplift you during this challenging time.

RACHEL'S REFLECTIONS & REMINDERS

1. Understand that it's okay to set boundaries and take a break from certain relationships during your grieving process. Protect your emotional well-being by limiting interactions with people who may not be sensitive or supportive.

2. Listen to your instincts and feelings about specific individuals. If someone's words or actions cause you distress during this vulnerable time, it's alright to temporarily step back from the relationship in a kind and loving way.

3. Use one-liners or gentle communication to express your need for space and time to grieve and heal. Politely let people know that you appreciate their heart and concern, but you need some personal time for yourself right now.

4. If you feel comfortable, share with others how they can better support you during this challenging time. Provide specific suggestions or resources they can use to be more helpful and compassionate.

5. While you give yourself space, remain open to reconnecting with people when you feel more emotionally resilient. Remember that this pause is temporary and doesn't necessarily mean ending the relationship altogether.

6.4

THE BEST OF OUR ABILITY VERSUS PERFECTIONISM, PERFORMANCE, AND PROCRASTINATION

Grief is work. Avoiding grief is more work.

DAVID KESSLER[20]

Perfection, performance, and procrastination are the three Ps that can sneak their way into your life while you are grieving and healing if you are not looking out for them. They show up in our relationships with ourselves and others, sometimes subtly, sometimes sneakily, and often unnoticed when we are traveling life on autopilot.

What do these three Ps look like:

- Perfectionism can look like carrying about your daily life like nothing significant has happened to you when we both know that's not the truth.

- Performance can look like taking on that extra meeting your boss suggested when you know you are at your maximum capacity.

- Procrastination can look like telling a friend you will find a support group but putting it off until you are in crisis mode and no longer have a choice in the matter.

133

Each of these Ps is really a symptom of avoidance.

Avoidance can look like telling yourself you will go to the grocery store to buy some healthy foods your body so desperately needs and then not doing it for days because you can't bear to be out where people might ask you why your sweet one is not with you. (Note: sometimes avoidance is necessary at the beginning of your grief journey, but other times it's not.)

You know these terms well and can think of examples of how they might appear in your life, and I don't want to bore you with this topic. I simply bring it to your awareness as they became part of my grief journey and countless clients' journeys.

I've found that giving ourselves grace, mercy, and kindness just as we would someone else in our shoes will enhance our self-respect and confidence in our ability to care for ourselves and give us breathing room when expectations, demands, or obligations are upon us.

Some of us find it difficult to function at any level of grief. Our brains are not working, and we can't stop crying. Sometimes, you can muster up the energy to get out of the house; other days, you will simply do your best.

I suggest keeping this one-liner in your back pocket for situations and circumstances when you must advocate for yourself and be your own best friend: "I appreciate your request or suggestion; however, today is one of those days where I'm already operating at capacity. Thank you for your grace."

When your family member, friend, or a close coworker asks you to go to lunch with them because you "need some fresh air and cheering up," you can say, "I love you, and I love the way you love me. Right now, I'm not in a place emotionally where I want to be out with people and have conversations."

If you need to explain further, you could follow that up with, "I know you trust that I know what's best for me. Thank you for respecting my turning down your thoughtful invitation. I want you to know I look forward to taking you up on your offer in a few days. Now let me go back to bed!"

This is precisely what I told my husband one day after Winston passed, and it's okay to say it.

Thank you, my beloved friend, for allowing me to speak on a topic I'm sure you wrestle with regularly. My heart desires to equip you with the awareness and the tools for potential stumbling blocks as you navigate this tsunami we call grief.

Remember, there is no one way or right way to grieve, and healing is a personal and unique process. Be patient with yourself as you navigate through the challenges of grief, and know that it's okay to do things to the best of your ability, even if they may not meet the expectations of others.

Your healing journey is about honoring your emotions, embracing self-compassion, and taking the necessary steps to move forward at your own pace.

RACHEL'S REFLECTIONS & REMINDERS

1. Recognize your limits and set achievable goals for yourself. Avoid taking on more than you can handle, and prioritize self-care and healing over performance.

2. Celebrate your progress on your healing journey instead of striving for perfection. Small steps forward are significant achievements. Perfection is unattainable in all things.

3. Recognize when you procrastinate and identify the underlying reasons. Address any fears or anxieties that may be causing avoidance.

4. Communicate your emotional state and needs to others. Let them know when you need space, support, or understanding.

5. Don't be afraid to accept help from others. Surround yourself with a supportive network of people who understand your situation.

CHAPTER SEVEN

ADJUSTING TO A NEW NORMAL

DON'T GET RID OF THEIR STUFF QUITE YET

Little by little we manage to let go of loss,
but we never let go of love.

UNKNOWN

I will never forget the anguish and remorse one woman was going through when she shared in one of my pet loss support groups that she threw away all of her dog's toys, beds, food, and essentially all of her dog's belongings.

She did it because she couldn't bear seeing his belongings all over her house, so in a frantic state of crying, she decided the best thing to do was to get rid of it all because he was no longer with her and it was too painful for her heart. But here she sat, bawling because she couldn't believe all traces of him were gone so soon.

I bet you can relate to part or all of her story. Hers is a natural reaction to a painful situation. We don't do things perfectly, and we can imagine that being in this situation would be so debilitating and confusing.

She thought she would be helping herself by eliminating the things that were causing her to miss her sweet boy even more. The constant reminder that he would never sleep in his favorite worn-out bed, throw his toys up in the air and catch them to make her laugh, or go for a spirited walk in the flashy collar and leash she bought him a year ago was just too painful.

The grief she felt is only some people's shared experience, though. Others are at peace with donating or removing their sweet one's belongings immediately. Every road to recovery is different, and it's crucial that we not judge ourselves or others for doing what they think they need to do.

I often suggest to my clients who call me immediately after their beloved dies not to throw anything out just yet. I explain that it takes some time for the shock to dissipate so they can once again think clearly.

Regrets of things done in haste and emotional overload are hard to overcome. In fact, regrets are one of the biggest stumbling blocks on our road to recovery, so the fewer regrets we can prevent after the loss, the better.

If seeing the cherished belongings of your pet is too painful right now, I suggest you—or someone close to you—carefully place them in a box in a closet or somewhere out of sight where you feel comfortable keeping them. This allows you the space you may need now from seeing those items and feeling even sadder.

The good thing about this plan is you can always bring the box back out any time in those moments you want to feel close to them through their physical items. It also allows you some time to decide whether you'd like to keep them, donate them, or throw them away when you are ready. The choice will be yours because you decided to keep them until your mind and heart know exactly what to do.

To say a word about donation, many shelters might like to have some of your washed and cared for items or unopened food, and some vets are happy to take back unused medicine.

I have found that many of my clients decide to keep most of their sweet one's belongings for a new love they may welcome in their home and heart one day. And you, like many others, can keep them for yourself forever.

There is no pressure, judgment, or right or wrong thing to do here.

I encourage you to make your grief and healing journey a self-honoring one by being patient with yourself. Try not to make hasty decisions that you might regret down the road. And please remember, there is no right way or one way to do this grief thing. Take the time you need to do it in a way that feels right to you.

You control how you want to remember your sweet one, and I'm here to support you.

RACHEL'S REFLECTIONS & REMINDERS

1. Regret can be a significant hurdle in the healing process. Avoid unnecessary regrets by holding off on getting rid of your sweet one's belongings until you feel more emotionally stable and clear-headed.

2. If seeing your pet's belongings is too painful at the moment, consider placing them in a room, closet, or designated storage area where you feel comfortable keeping them. You can bring them out whenever you're ready to feel close to your sweet one through their physical items.

3. With time, you may donate some of their belongings to a veterinary office, shelter, or rescue or even share some toys with a friend's pet. These acts can help create positive memories and benefit other animals in need.

4. Many people keep most of their pet's belongings, especially if they plan to welcome a new pet into their home one day. Holding onto these items can help keep the memory of your sweet one alive.

5. Hold onto the love and cherished memories you shared with your sweet one. Their belongings can remind you of the beautiful bond you had, and you can decide when the right time is to let go or preserve those mementos.

REPURPOSE STUFF

I don't think of all the misery, but of all the beauty that remains.

BRUCE F. SINGER[21]

What a brilliant idea," I said to my client. "I love how your mom inspired you to turn one of Scooby's toys into a Christmas tree ornament!"

It warms my heart to hear the incredibly thoughtful, clever, and purposeful ways in which my clients come up with fantastic ways to repurpose their precious pets' belongings for their families to enjoy for a lifetime.

Some clients will even leave their sweet ones' nose prints on their car windows for a while; this is one I hear often. I suggest they take a photo or place tape on the window to capture the print and make it into art.

I also often hear cat parents share how they don't want to vacuum up their sweet ones' hair from the carpet or rug because that will officially be the last essence of them in the house. I suggest that they vacuum and collect the hair and make a small pillow or something special out of it or find something creative and meaningful to do with it.

These are just a few examples, as there are so many ways you can sentimentally repurpose your sweet ones' things if you so desire.

When Winston passed, Simon and I decided to make a tribute and celebration of life area for Winston's ashes in our formal living room. It felt right. We have his leash and collar, a beautiful wooden box with his ashes, one of his toys, and a painting of him on top of a beautiful buffet hutch. We also officially gave his brother, Spencer, some of Winston's toys because we did not want to take them from Spencer.

It was hard to see them sitting in their toy box without Winston being there to pull them out and strategically place them around the house, but we knew keeping them was the right thing to do for Spencer.

I did, however, throw out some of Winston's beds. I could not handle seeing them without him. You just have to determine what you can and can't handle, what can be repurposed, and what needs to go.

If you want to keep some of your loved ones' things, I encourage you to keep an open mind and get creative in making them a part of your new life without your pet.

My friend, you will get through this and won't regret having some keepsakes for years as an excellent way to remember them. Repurposing your pet's belongings in these creative ways can help you preserve their memory and hold a special place in your heart. Embrace the memories and find solace in the unique and thoughtful ways you can honor your beloved pet's legacy.

RACHEL'S REFLECTIONS & REMINDERS

1. Inspired by my client's idea of turning one of Scooby's toys into a Christmas tree ornament, I encourage others to do the same. Select a special toy with sentimental value and transform it into a cherished decoration for the holiday season.

2. Consider creating a memory keepsake quilt using your pet's old blankets or favorite fabric. Cut the fabric into squares and sew them together to make a cozy quilt that will serve as a beautiful reminder of your furry friend and keep their essence close to you.

3. Instead of letting your pet's hair go to waste, transform it into meaningful jewelry. You can find artisans who specialize in crafting custom pet hair jewelry. Whether it's a necklace, bracelet, or even a keychain, having a piece of jewelry made from your pet's hair can be a unique and sentimental way to always carry their memory with you.

4. Create a tribute table or a celebration of life area in your home. This area can include items like a collar, leash, favorite toy, a beautiful box with ashes, and even a painting or photograph of your sweet one. (I have one in my home and my home office.) Be creative, and remember to check out my website for resources and inspiration.

5. When multiple pets are in your household, some toys may hold memories of the departed pet. You can pass these toys to the surviving pets to honor the memory of their lost companion and comfort your remaining pets.

7.3

TAKE BABY STEPS

What we once enjoyed and deeply loved we can never
lose, for all that we deeply love becomes a part of us.

CARON B. GOODE[22]

I know grieving is the last thing you want to do in life. You want this to
have never happened in the first place. The passing of your beloved pet
has created a new reality that seems too hard to imagine. I get it, my friend.
But there is hope!

You are taking the first step in creating a healing environment and healthy
support system to carry you through this grief journey. Right now, an opportunity presents itself for you to care for yourself like never before.

When Winston passed, I had a choice just as you do today. I could resist what
was happening in my little world or open my heart to take baby steps toward
this new and unwanted reality—one I could live with and eventually thrive in.

I had several defining points to make choices about my new reality throughout my day. I could wake up in the morning and feel like I wanted to be
depressed and stay in bed all day, blowing off my responsibilities, or I could
ask my husband if I could talk with him for a few minutes and share the
dream I just had about our sweet boy.

I could avoid the kitchen altogether because looking at where Winston
would be having breakfast with us broke my shattered heart into even more
pieces, or I could sit on the floor where his bowls were and talk to his spirit,

sharing how much I miss him already and telling him that our home will never be the same without him.

I could skip going for an evening walk right before bed because it hurt so much not to have him on the leash beside me, or I could be brave enough to go outside and sit on the porch and talk to him as I look up at the stars, knowing he is watching over us.

These are just a few examples of how I decided to take baby steps toward a new normal. This took work. This sucked. This hurt. And this took courage. But I did it anyway.

Four years later, my husband and I still do some of the same things we implemented into our lives when the pain of Winston's loss revisits. And I can tell you it works; it really works.

When you are faced with adjusting to a new normal, consider adding something special to your old routine, taking one step at a time. If you fed your sweet one at certain times, think about how to turn that into prayer time or whatever feels like you are honoring your sweet one.

Doing this does take work and practice. It will pay off in the long run because you intentionally added unique elements to your old routine. My beloved, taking baby steps in creating a new routine and adjusting to a new normal will help you have some control over what has happened to you and your family with the loss of your sweet one.

You may have more time on your hands than before. If so, add some rest and relaxation to your routine. There is no better time than now to do this.

Remember, these suggestions are just that: suggestions. They will not erase your pain or change how you feel. But they will impact your healing journey as you make healthy decisions that lead to healing your heart with perseverance, courage, and grace.

Healing is a process unique to each individual, and it's okay to take the time you need to find your new normal. Your beloved pet will always hold a special place in your heart, and the healing journey is about learning to carry their memory with love and grace.

RACHEL'S REFLECTIONS & REMINDERS

1. Adjusting to a new normal takes time. Take small steps to incorporate changes into your daily routine that honor the memory of your sweet one and help you cope with the loss.

2. Consider turning old routines into special rituals to honor your pet's memory. For example, if you used to feed them at certain times, use those moments as opportunities for prayer or reflection.

3. Spend time outdoors, connect with nature, and find solace in its beauty. Feeling closer to your pet's spirit and finding peace can be comforting.

4. It's essential to be patient with yourself as you navigate through this challenging time. Treat yourself with the same compassion you would offer to a friend going through a loss.

5. Surround yourself with positive influences, whether uplifting books, supportive friends, or inspiring stories of others who have overcome grief.

7.4

EMBRACE YOUR NEW IDENTITY

Life has to end. Love doesn't.

MITCH ALBOM[23]

S ee the tall blonde over there; that's Winston's Mom." I heard this at our
vet's office one day, and it occurred to me that other dog people I know,
and even some neighbors, know me as Winston's mom.

I bet you can relate.

You may not have been conscious of it until reading this, but there is something so sweet and wonderful about hearing our names be replaced with our
beloved pets' names and then Mom or Dad after it. I would not trade this
identity for anything.

I wish I were still called Winston's Mom today, but I am grateful to be
called Spencer and Charley's Mom. Let's face it: until the day God calls me
home to heaven, I will be called some sweet angel's mom.

In fact, it is my secret desire to one day have a senior dog rescue farm here
in the Carolinas where I live now, and then I will be called the mom of whatever we name the place, God willing.

But back to you, my love. If you haven't already, you will probably run
into neighbors, friends, acquaintances, fellow pet parents, vets, groomers,
pet sitters, people you would see while on vacation with your sweet angel,

restaurant patrons, and coffee shop owners (fill in the blank for you), and they might not even know your first name and still want to address you as your sweet one's Mom or Dad.

I know it was an absolute honor to be their mom or dad. It was one of the best labels you could imagine in a world that loves to label people for what they are and are not. No label could be better positioned in our hearts than the name Mom or Dad of our sweet ones.

The tension happens when we hold on to this welcomed identity for too long after our sweet one dies. The choice is whether to let people know what your real name is and if you still want to be addressed by what they know to call you.

Earlier in this book, I talked about how helpful one-liners are to have in your pocket for different scenarios you will encounter on your grieving journey. One-liners are great for these situations, too. Find the phrasing that works best for you.

My encouragement is for you to recognize if running into these lovely people brings up too much pain, knowing that you will need to let them know your sweet one has passed, and "Oh, by the way, my name is _____, but it would be just fine with me if you still call me her Mom because I always will be." The other option is to say, "Oh, by the way, my name is _____. What's yours?" You may have already run into this scenario and didn't know what to do. This is just an example of some verbiage to help you formulate what resonates with your heart in your communication with others.

Here's another example: You run into someone at a coffee shop who is used to seeing you with your sweet one, and they ask where they are. You can reply with something like, "It's great to see you too. Yes, Petey is not with me because he went to heaven recently. Thank you for understanding I'm not in a place to share more right now, but I want you to know how much I appreciate your prayers and support as I take time to heal from this loss." And then change the subject. "So, how have you and your family been doing?" Or you can shut down the conversation with, "I look forward to seeing you next time."

I encourage you to find the words that best suit your personality and communication style. Just have a few one-liners ready for different situations.

Some people will contact you on social media looking for those precious and funny photos they are used to seeing of you documenting your sweet pet's life as they live like a queen or king.

If you have a static answer in place, you'll manage those emotions better than having to come up with something that brings up a lot of feelings at an inopportune time.

The bottom line is that often, your identity has been associated with your amazing pet, so people will unknowingly label you as such unless you turn that uncomfortable moment around and decide how you want to be addressed moving forward. Regardless of how you choose to handle those initial social situations, you'll need to find ways to make peace with your new identity.

You can choose how you want to show up and participate in life while grieving. You can think about how you want to be known and who you are becoming at this pivotal point in your life.

My encouragement is to embrace your new identity with dignity, grace, and grit because the world needs you, my beloved friend.

And remember, it's natural to feel a mix of emotions as you embrace your new identity after losing your pet. Allow yourself the freedom to grieve, explore, and grow, knowing that your love for your sweet one will always be a cherished part of who you are.

RACHEL'S REFLECTIONS & REMINDERS

1. Develop one-liners or responses that help you gracefully navigate conversations when others refer to you as your pet's Mom or Dad. Find words that honor your sweet one's memory while gently informing others of their passing.

2. It's okay to let people know if discussing your pet's passing is too painful for you at the moment. Set boundaries on what you're comfortable sharing and allow yourself time to heal.

3. Take this time to explore hobbies, activities, or interests you may have set aside while caring for your pet. Rediscover passions that bring you joy and fulfillment.

4. Be patient and compassionate with yourself as you navigate this period of transition. Allow yourself time to grieve and find comfort in your own way.

5. Recognize the resilience and strength you have shown throughout your grief journey. Embrace your capacity to grow and evolve while carrying your sweet one's memory in your heart.

7.5

CREATE A SAFE PLACE
FOR MELTDOWNS

There is a sacredness in tears. They are not the mark of
weakness, but of power. They speak more eloquently than ten
thousand tongues. They are the messengers of overwhelming
grief, of deep contrition, and of unspeakable love.

JOHN BATE[24]

When my husband brought our sweet boy Winston's ashes home from our vet's office, it was hard to see him in a wooden box tucked nicely in a bag. I asked Simon if he could put the bag somewhere while I gathered some courage.

When I stopped uncontrollably crying and shaking, I asked Simon if he was ready to open the bag. Together, we put the bag on top of the living room buffet cabinet, gently opened it with tears running down our faces, and said a prayer.

We asked God for His strength and a sense of peace in our broken hearts so that we could do the next right thing and place Winston in his final resting place here at home with us.

Simon pulled the box from the bag and placed it on the cabinet. He pulled out Winston's paw print that the vet made as a keepsake for us and then a lock of Winston's fur in a clear bag with a purple bow. There was a beautiful card from our vet's office and Winston's collar and leash that Simon also took out of the bag.

I remember clearly how I felt in that strange moment. Seeing our boy's body reduced to ashes in a box, a paw print, and a lock of fur was a very sad moment.

We made a special place right on that hutch for his beautiful wooden urn, his paw print in clay, and his collar and leash. We decided right then that's where Winston's remains would live.

I was not able to have his lock of fur out. I had to keep it in the bag with the card because it was too much of a visual reminder of him. I promptly took the bag and placed it in my closet.

I think God guided me to my closet, knowing this would be my new safe place away from the world, my husband, my other pup (Spencer), my home office, and everything else so I could have as many meltdowns as I wanted.

I thank God for guiding me there because for quite some time after Winston passed, I used it countless times to spend time with Winston and cry my eyes out.

I always share this story with my clients to illuminate and illustrate the importance of creating a safe place for you to have meltdowns.

You may not have considered this before, but having a designated place allows you privacy and safety in those moments when you just need to release but want to do it alone. Many people are afraid to feel their feelings, and safe places away from the prying eyes or fragile hearts of others let us get to our real feelings and fully experience them. Crying is cathartic and is meant to be healing when we let it be.

Do you have a place where you can be alone in your home? It might be a closet, the bathroom, the basement, or simply a room in which you feel free to close the door. You can bring some of your pet's belongings in with you. You could keep a journal there, or maybe you would benefit from having a weighted blanket or a stuffed animal to hold on to while crying. Whatever works best for you is just fine.

I simply advise you to make a space that allows you to feel your feelings fully without any expectations that you must hold "it" together. Your grief and healing journey will benefit significantly from this.

Remember, your safe place is a space for you to process your grief and emotions authentically. It's a sanctuary for healing, and embracing this space can help you navigate the ups and downs of the grieving process with more resilience and self-compassion.

RACHEL'S REFLECTIONS & REMINDERS

1. Find a quiet and private space in your home where you can retreat when you need to have a meltdown. This could be a specific room or a cozy closet spot—somewhere you feel safe and undisturbed.

2. Make the safe place your own by adding items that bring comfort and evoke positive memories of your beloved pet. This could include photos, mementos, or any sentimental objects.

3. Understand that meltdowns are a natural part of the grieving process. Give yourself permission to feel and express your emotions without judgment or pressure to be strong.

4. Establish a simple ritual that helps you center yourself before and after a meltdown. It could be deep breathing exercises, lighting a candle, or praying.

5. Don't rush the process. Give yourself as much time as you need during each meltdown session. Let your emotions flow naturally, and avoid putting pressure on yourself to get over it.

CHAPTER EIGHT

PAYING IT FORWARD (LEGACY)

LEGACY IDEAS
TO CONTEMPLATE

What you do is your history. What you set in motion is your legacy.

LEONARD SWEET[25]

The word legacy has a significant meaning to me. When I first became a professional coach, the word was rarely used.

I first thought about the word and its importance while I was training to become a coach. We were looking at all the different niches or ways we could help, and the one that no one looked at but leaped off the page and penetrated my heart was a legacy coach.

Wow, I thought, *this is precisely what I want to help people uncover, discover, and create because that is how God designed me at the center of my being. My DNA is all about not dying with our music still in us and paying it forward to help others.*

But how does that relate to you? Legacy matters, so your sweet one's legacy matters.

You, me, and our sweet ones were not created by our Heavenly Father just to wander around this planet trying to survive the years we are meant to live here. We are here to positively contribute to the people, places, animals, and things that are brought into our lives in one way or another.

All of this points back with gratitude, honor, and glory to the one who created us, our lives, and our world. Your sweet one's life and the life you shared were precious and significant and not for nothing. If it resonates with your spirit, you have a glorious opportunity to celebrate your sweet one's life.

You may be thinking that your pet was just a regular, sweet, loving pet with no significant contribution or extraordinary talents that the world witnessed. You may be right, but they did make significant contributions. I bet they impacted you and influenced how you showed up in the world.

Perhaps they inspired and aided you in becoming a more loving human being, taught you how to forgive quickly, or helped you to have fun in the most unusual ways. You see where I'm going here. The lessons you learned are priceless teachable moments for someone in your sphere of influence and maybe even the world.

If this resonates with you, here are a few ideas to get you started as you contemplate some legacy ideas because it's all about paying it forward with dignity, grace, and love.

You could start a blog writing to those who also had to make the hard decision to euthanize their sweet one because of aggressive behavior or for those who got a pet from a puppy mill that ended up in an awful situation. You could write about how to avoid adoption scams because you were scammed or write to fellow agility trainers about what made your pet a superstar. Write about how the veterinary community has one of the highest suicide rates, and you and your sweet one absolutely loved your veterinarian and the veterinarian community, so you find purpose in writing about this topic to bring awareness and solutions.

You can see that even thinking about blogging, speaking, or starting a non-profit in your sweet one's name can change your world and our world, one meaningful sweet one's legacy at a time. You could plant trees in your area because your boy loved peeing on trees; it was his way of watering them because he cared so much about the planet.

I'm being silly here, but it's true, isn't it? When you think about your pet and his or her special idiosyncrasies, I bet ways to remember them and perpetuate their legacy will start coming to mind. Uncovering, discovering, and creating a legacy is a beautiful way to give back and pay it forward. I can't wait to hear what clever legacy ideas and plans you come up with, my love!

Remember that contemplating and creating a legacy is a personal and heartfelt process. Let your heart guide you. Whatever legacy ideas you pursue will be the right ones for you.

RACHEL'S REFLECTIONS & REMINDERS

1. Take time to reflect on how your sweet one positively impacted your life. Consider the lessons they taught you, the love they shared, and the unique qualities they possessed.

2. Remember that every pet's legacy is unique, just like they were. Your sweet one may not have achieved worldwide fame or recognition, but their impact on your life and those around you is precious and meaningful. Embrace the individuality of their legacy.

3. Come up with creative ways to honor your pet's memory and share their legacy. Writing a blog, creating a website, starting a podcast, or even writing a book can be a powerful way to express your feelings, share valuable insights, and connect with others who have had similar experiences.

4. Consider advocating for causes that are close to your heart. It could be related to animal welfare, pet health, or any other topic that aligns with their journey. Raising awareness and making a difference in these areas can be a meaningful tribute.

5. Consider donating to or volunteering with animal welfare organizations or charities that align with your pet's legacy. Supporting these causes can positively impact the lives of animals in need and contribute to a more compassionate world.

START A NEW TRADITION

When you serve others, when you make somebody else's life better, when you lift up people, when you help heal those that are hurting, not only are they being blessed, but you're being blessed.

JOEL OSTEEN[26]

A dear friend named Jim sent me the most thoughtful gift when he learned that our beloved Winston had passed. It was a beautiful condolence card with a note sharing that Jim made a donation to our local animal shelter in Winston's honor. As the tears flowed from my eyes, I couldn't help but reflect on the love and insightful care I received from my precious friend Jim.

To this day, I have adopted this beautifully sentimental way of giving a condolence gift to my friends and families when their pet passes. I also share this with my clients as an example of what you can do to create a new tradition of honoring your sweet one.

Just because you are creating a new life without your sweet one doesn't mean it needs to be a life void of their memory altogether. You can get creative about remembering them by implementing something new and meaningful into a tradition that feels honoring, loving, and purposeful.

You could also make a donation at your friend's local shelter, volunteer at your local shelter, help raise awareness for a cause that was important to you and your sweet one, or start a blog sharing with the world the beautiful lessons you learned over the years from your sweet one. These are just a few ideas, but there are so many to choose from.

If you want to do something like this but aren't sure what might be best for you, I suggest you spend some time brainstorming, talking with a friend or family member, or making a list of pros and cons for your different ideas. I'm confident you will develop something that feels right for you.

By incorporating something special and new into your life that honors your pet's memory, you open up your life and heart to new opportunities, possibilities, and miracles. What a gift in the midst of heartache!

Consider this: grieving can be a dreadful time in your life, and it can be an insightful time in your life. I encourage you to reach for something insightful that both mends your pain and allows you to be creative and give to others. The possibilities of a new, rewarding, and honoring way of doing this thing called grief are endless—if you'll only try. You can do this! I know it.

And remember, there is no right or wrong way to honor your beloved pet. Choose the actions that resonate most deeply with your personality and resources and feel authentic to your bond with your sweet one.

By incorporating these new traditions and acts of love, you can find comfort and meaning as you navigate the grieving process and carry your pet's memory in your heart.

RACHEL'S REFLECTIONS & REMINDERS

1. Consider making a donation to a local animal shelter or a pet-related charity in your pet's memory. This act of kindness helps animals in need and honors the love you shared with your sweet one.

2. Share the beautiful memories and life lessons you learned from your sweet one by starting a journal or a blog. Writing about your experiences can be therapeutic and may help others who are going through a similar grieving process.

3. Consider gathering friends and family who have lost pets and create a special remembrance day to celebrate the lives of all the beloved animals you've lost together.

4. Join pet-related events or walks that support animal causes. Participating in these events can be a meaningful way to remember your pet while connecting with others who share similar sentiments.

5. Carry on your pet's legacy of love and kindness by performing acts of kindness for animals and pet owners in need.

HELPING OTHERS HELPS YOU

Those who are happiest are those who do the most for others.

BROOKER T. WASHINGTON[27]

One of the best ways to get our minds off our problems is to help others in their time of need. Actually, it does not matter if they are in need or not. The only requirement in knowing if we should help others is if they are still breathing.

Honestly, I think one of the many reasons God designed us to care for one another is because it's a clever way to distract us from our worries and woes. He knows how much we think about ourselves and can become preoccupied and consumed with what we think and what others think about us. This is one of the reasons why my love language is paying it forward.

Being legacy-driven is in my DNA. A genuine concern for others leaves a lasting impression on the hearts of those we bless with our time, talents, and treasures. Having this heart posture sets an example and invites those around us to become aware of how they, too, can make a meaningful contribution and difference as well.

Many clients ask me for suggestions on making the ache in their hearts stop hurting so much, and I affectionately respond by encouraging them to get busy helping others. Obviously, this is not the sole way to ease your heart's ache.

Hopefully, this book has illuminated a lot of helpful ideas for you. Still, serving sure does open up opportunities; otherwise, it is not even on the radar to take your mind off your circumstances and pass it on to those who can benefit from your experience, strength, humility, hope, and acts of kindness.

As I mentioned before, please understand that when I share a glimpse of the lessons I've learned and implemented in life—some easily with an open heart and others painfully with resistance but learned and applied nonetheless—it's to come alongside you and lift you up and help sustain you on your road to recovery.

Having a teachable spirit brings about the most divine healing and rewarding life. We don't do things perfectly, but we do them with the intention and satisfaction of sleeping well at night, knowing we gave that day our best shot. And it will be easier to get out of bed and serve others on some days than others. This is all normal and understandable.

Now, as for how to serve others or what to do, you have seen and read lists of ways you can help others, so I won't bore you with another list.

Here's the deal though: ask God each day to show you who needs some encouragement and who will benefit from a random ask of kindness from you today, and you'll be set. See how many days in a row you can do this and feel your heart lighten up.

That would be a great place to start. Eventually, you can perhaps serve someone or in some organization more easily. And when you don't know what to do, remember that even giving a smile is encouraging, and you can treat your random act of kindness as your secret agent mission and make some fun of it. I promise you will find the energy to be a secret agent because it's so dang fun.

The bottom line is to intentionally do what you can to create an atmosphere where you can experience and cherish miracles even in times of turmoil and tribulation but, most importantly, help you stay others-focused rather than getting caught up in self-pity. Giving to others can be a way of life if you make it a core value of your heart.

I'm not suggesting we do these things for admiration, attention, recognition, or selfish ambition. Instead, it's for legacy-driven connection and contribution. The world needs you, my beloved friend; it's time.

Remember that helping others is a selfless act that can be incredibly fulfilling and healing. As you focus on uplifting those around you, you may find your heart lightening up and your perspective on life shifting in a positive direction. Embrace the power of giving and continue cultivating an atmosphere of love, kindness, and contribution.

RACHEL'S REFLECTIONS & REMINDERS

1. When you are preoccupied with your worries and woes, consciously shift your focus to helping others. Redirecting your attention to someone else's needs can provide a sense of purpose and fulfillment.

2. You don't have to undertake grand gestures to make a difference. Small acts of kindness and compassion can significantly impact someone's day and create a ripple effect of positivity.

3. Take a moment each day to pray or meditate, asking for guidance on how to help others. Trust that opportunities will present themselves when you are open to them.

4. By embodying a life of giving and compassion, you can inspire those around you to do the same. Lead by example and encourage others to join in the journey of helping others.

5. Celebrate the small victories and sweet moments of joy that come from helping others. Acknowledge the positive changes you've made in someone's life, and let it motivate you to continue your legacy-driven efforts.

YOUR TEST BECOMES YOUR TESTIMONY AND LIVING LEGACY

One truly must have suffered oneself to help others.

MOTHER TERESA[28]

I have said this throughout the book, and if you were my client, you'd hear it a lot in our time together as well, but it's worth repeating often. Your healing and grief journey is precisely that: a journey.

I prefer to look at roads we travel as journeys rather than destinations. Destinations have a beginning and an end, while journeys can start one way and turn another. We can take time on our journey to rest, reflect, and renew our sense of purpose. We also can push pause, pivot, and pray for a new direction.

What you are going through will help someone in the future. You can turn what feels like a terrifying tragedy into a triumphant testimony. This is a testing time, my friend. Your grief will test your courage and character, resulting in some of the most valuable insights, lessons, and wisdom as your journey will eventually shift into another season.

Because of this, you will see how resilient and courageous you have become and how your experience can be the light to someone else's darkest hour. Your test will become your testimony.

I know you didn't ask for this test, nor is it one you want to go through. I understand. It's hard to navigate unwanted journeys through life. I empathize with you and am here to help you carry on.

One of the best tools I reach for when I've identified God has me in a testing situation or season is the Serenity Prayer.

It goes without saying that you may already be familiar with this, as I affectionately call it, the "keep things in perspective prayer;" however, I encourage you to read it often, say it out loud or under your breath, specifically the extended version below:

> God grant me the serenity to accept the things I cannot change, the courage to change the things I can, and the wisdom to know the difference, living one day at a time, enjoying one moment at a time, taking this world as it is and not as I would have it; trusting that You will make all things right if I surrender to Your will; so that I may be reasonably happy in this life and supremely happy with You forever in the next. Amen.[29]

As you meditate on this helpful prayer, remember the people who shared their testimonies with you as a reminder that you will persevere. They came into your life, and you will soon be able to do the same for someone else.

Take time, my beloved friend, and always remember you have the power to turn this test into a testimony. Remember your story, experiences, and journey are unique and valuable. By sharing your testimony and living with purpose, you can touch the lives of others and leave a meaningful legacy of hope, strength, and resilience.

RACHEL'S REFLECTIONS AND REMINDERS

1. Recognize that what you are going through has the potential to help others in the future. Your experiences and how you overcome challenges can become a source of inspiration and support for others facing similar situations.

2. Reframe your perspective on your experiences. Instead of viewing them as terrifying tragedies, look for opportunities to turn them into triumphant testimonies. Your ability to find strength in difficult times can be a powerful message of hope for others.

3. Consider sharing your testimony with others through writing, speaking, or connecting with individuals facing similar challenges. Your willingness to be vulnerable and authentic can create a profound impact.

4. Reflect on the quote from Mother Teresa, "One truly must have suffered oneself to help others." Recognize that your own experiences of pain and suffering can deepen your understanding and empathy for others in need.

5. Draw strength from the stories of people who have shared their testimonies with you. Recognize that just as they came into your life and made a difference, you have the potential to do the same for someone else.

CHAPTER NINE

TIME TO LOVE AGAIN

9.1

YOU CAN LOVE AGAIN

The purpose of life, after all, is to live it, to taste
experience to the utmost, to reach out eagerly and
without fear for newer and richer experience.

ELEANOR ROOSEVELT[30]

I often hear pet parents say they could not imagine ever having another pet because it hurts too much to lose them. They aptly describe their pain as feeling devastated, debilitated, and absolutely crushed.

They had their heart ripped out of their chest and had never felt this much pain. They've even said this pain is worse than when their parent died. Everyone responds differently, but the pain is equally deep and heart-wrenching.

I hear these things daily from beloved pet parents like you. I can tell you that the pain, despair, and heartache get better as you begin to feel supported, cared for, listened to, honored, and respected while you mourn in your own unique way.

That's why supporting you and others in this way is an honor. It's also a blessing and privilege to help you see what could be after all that has been lost. You have the authority, power, and responsibility to choose if and when you will contemplate and potentially welcome a new bundle of love into your life. Period. You are in charge and can trust yourself to know what's best for you and your family.

That said, I will share with you what I share with my clients. I have learned that God designed us to nurture. When you view yourself as a devoted pet parent, you separate yourself from other pet parents who may simply view animals as just that: animals.

That is their view, and I'm not judging them; I'm just distinguishing a viewpoint difference. You know the difference I'm speaking of, right? There are people with pets, and then there are pet parents.

God designed us, devoted pet parents, as an army of His most treasured animal lovers who see animals as He does: as beautiful, special, and priceless. Even though you are grieving now, that doesn't mean you have lost your inherent instinct to take care of and nurture a sweet one again—and possibly a few more in your lifetime.

You and I know we could never replace the life and love we lost. There is no way physically, emotionally, spiritually, relationally, or energetically. You continue to love them without their physical bodies being here. Maybe even more now that they are gone. Considering welcoming a new love into your life would never replace what you had with your beloved pet that passed. You are not alone in this thinking. It's very common to feel the way you do. "Death leaves a heartache no one can heal, love leaves a memory no one can steal."[31]

Perspective is everything. When we are experiencing the most painful loss we have ever experienced up to this point in our lives, it's not the best time to make big decisions until some space and time have allowed our minds to think clearly about the future.

I encourage you to become fluid when making decisions, knowing it's okay to change your mind and then change it again. As you are experiencing, this journey is a windy road, not a straight one. I remind you of this because I desire what's best for you, my love.

But when you are ready, I encourage you to open your heart and mind to welcome and not deny love to another sweet one. Countless pets alive today and born soon could use a soft landing place right in your heart and home.

We are not here to save all the animals, just the ones God places on our hearts and delivers to us in the most extraordinary and clever ways.

When asked about this topic, my heart leaps for joy because I enjoy shining light on what can happen when you say yes again. Many people, including me, love adopting from a shelter or rescue.

I share with you and my clients that if you feel called to bring a beautiful puppy, kitten, horse, or your favorite type of pet and prefer to bring it home as a baby, that is more than okay.

I know many people may feel differently, but buying a pet from a breeder is more than okay. You are still rescuing that baby pet because you never know whose hands they could have gone to if not yours.

I suggest you research breeders, shelters, and rescues to ensure you don't inadvertently support something you would not want to, but in my opinion, all pets need a home—no matter where they come from before our home. Those baby kittens at a breeder need a home just as much as the sweet puppy that was left on the street.

They all need our love, so be kind to yourself and keep an open mind about whether welcoming and not denying love to you and another sweet one is right for you in the future or even today.

There is no pressure, judgment, or obligation to entertain my suggestion. I'm here to help you see all the possibilities that can and will enrich your life if you choose them.

For now, remain open until you have peace about the next level of nurturing you will invite into your heart and home. Trust how God made you and trust you will make the right decision when the time comes.

Remember that there is no rush or pressure to decide and no right or wrong way to navigate this process. Your heart knows what is best for you, and when you are ready, opening your heart to another sweet one can be a beautiful way to continue the legacy of love and companionship you shared with your previous pet.

RACHEL'S REFLECTIONS & REMINDERS

1. Recognize that your capacity for love and nurturing is still present, even amidst grief. As a devoted pet parent, you can provide a loving and caring home for another sweet one when you are ready.

2. Trust your instincts and listen to your heart when contemplating bringing another pet into your life. Pay attention to any inner nudges or signs that indicate you may be ready for a new bundle of love.

3. Explore adoption or rescue options if and when you feel ready. There are countless pets in shelters and rescues that need loving homes. Opening your heart to them can be a rewarding and fulfilling experience. And please don't feel pressure to rescue or adopt from a shelter or organization if your heart tells you it's time for a specific breed or age from a reputable and ethical breeder that you want to consider.

4. Understand that it's okay to feel uncertain or conflicted about the idea of having another pet. Be kind to yourself and allow the process of decision-making to unfold naturally. Welcoming a new pet does not diminish your love for your late companion. It's a testament to your love's depth and ability to open your heart to possibly loving another sweet one in the future.

5. When the time comes, trust yourself and embrace the peace that comes with your decision. Know that you will make the right choice for you and the sweet one you may welcome into your heart and home.

NAVIGATE YOUR TRUTH VERSUS WHAT OTHERS SAY

Even if others don't understand your grief, God does—and
He wants to assure you of His constant love and presence.

BILLY GRAHAM[32]

Not everyone will understand what you are going through, have been through, and will go through. And that is more than okay. It takes special individuals to care for, love, and be loved by God's pets. Others might not understand such a deep love.

We are not here to please people. We are here to live our lives to the best of our ability, to the fullest extent possible, and to pay it forward to those around us and those to come.

Today, and any day for that matter, is not the day to entertain other people's opinions, suggestions, and hunches from God unless you have asked, invited, or solicited them to have a say concerning your affairs.

I have seen, heard, and experienced firsthand what can often feel like or be described as a well-intended person coming off in a bullying manner as a matter of self-righteousness. Stick with me here.

Can you tell that I feel just a tad passionate about this topic of conversation and contemplation? Yes! Because, my love, you have a responsibility and obligation to take care of and protect your environment, thoughts, feelings, actions, words, heart, and healing to be victorious on this grief and healing journey.

Give yourself permission not to need to justify or explain what you are thinking and experiencing to anyone. The truth of your situation and your feelings about it are just that: yours. Your truth can be influenced and changed for sure. You are growing and evolving, but you are not remaining the person you were before your sweet one died.

People can say the darndest things. People will try to convince you that getting another pet right now is the absolute best thing because they did it, and it helped. Or that getting a pet from a rescue is the only way to go or you don't care about suffering animals as they do. Or that if you buy a pet from a breeder, you support bad backyard breeders. You can fill in the blank; I'm sure you have heard a few in your lifetime.

Your truth is yours alone. Be gentle with yourself, keep those good one-liners we talked about in your pocket for times such as these, and always remember to stick up for yourself in the most loving way possible because they will respect you and admire your self-awareness in more ways than you know.

Lead by example, my beloved friend; speak and know your truth and carry on. Remember that your truth and your healing journey are valuable and valid. Embrace your authenticity and know it's okay to prioritize your well-being above others' opinions. Trust yourself, and know that you have the strength to navigate your grief and healing journey in a way that honors your heart and soul.

RACHEL'S REFLECTIONS & REMINDERS

1. Trust your instincts and intuition. You know yourself and your needs better than anyone else. Follow what feels right for you without feeling pressured by others' expectations or suggestions.

2. Have one-liners or responses ready for situations when others may offer unsolicited advice. Politely assert your boundaries and express that you are navigating your journey in a way that feels right for you.

3. Show others how to respect and honor their own truth by demonstrating it in your life. Lead by example, and others may learn to respect your journey and trust their own inner wisdom.

4. Be open to growth and evolution as you navigate your truth. Your experiences may shape and change your perspectives, but ultimately, you know what is right for you.

5. Celebrate your authenticity and courage to live your truth despite what others may say or think. Embrace your unique path and honor your growth and healing process.

MAYBE YOUR SWEET ONE WOULD WANT YOU TO LOVE AGAIN

The [one] we lost will never be forgotten. They will continue to live in our hearts and memories, reminding us of the love and joy they brought into our lives.

UNKNOWN[33]

After Winston passed, Simon and I waited about five months before we knew it was time to welcome another bundle of love into our hearts and home. Spencer was lonely and only knew growing up with Winston. I was grieving for myself, and I was grieving for Spencer.

Some people are ready a lot sooner, but we waited five months because of some life situations that would have made it an unwise decision if we welcomed a new love any sooner. So we were patient with our mourning, healing, and the decision to begin the search for a new little love.

The real push for us was the realization that Winston would want us to love again. That's the kind of boy he was. He loved other dogs and enjoyed seeing us loving on other people's pups when out and about.

When my clients ask if they should get another pet, I often ask them what they think their sweet one that passed would say, and about 99% say, "Yes,

Fluffy would want me to love one of her kitty friends just like I loved her." And then there is the 1% who say, "No way; Max would never want me to love another the way I loved him."

When I hear this, I softly lean in and say, "I can understand and appreciate that, but just remember that if you ever change your mind, please know you will love the new one differently than your previous one. Every relationship is different, and that's a wonderful truth."

My friend, perhaps you are in the 1% who can't imagine loving again. I hope my affirmation and encouragement provide helpful consideration. But again, the choice is really yours.

When Spencer, the love of my life, besides God, Simon, and our new love, Charley, passes away sometime in the not-so-far-off distance, I know for a fact that he will want us to welcome another joy-filled pup into our lives because I have asked him and he said he does.

Yep, I talk to my dogs, and they answer me most of the time. What? Your dogs don't talk? That's weird!

Anyway, even if I didn't think I understood our boxer's doggie talk, I know within the depths of my soul that he would want me to care for and love other dogs for the rest of my life because it will be helping them and me. Our pets just get it.

These are just some things to think about when making your decision. And not making a decision right now is making a decision, so keep on keeping on, my beloved friend. You'll know what to do if and when the time comes.

Remember that every person's journey is unique, and the decision to love again is deeply personal. Allow yourself the privilege of navigating this process with patience, love, and openness, and trust that you will know what to do when the time is right for you.

RACHEL'S REFLECTIONS & REMINDERS

1. Reflect on the loving and compassionate nature of your sweet one who passed. Remember how they enjoyed seeing you love and care for other animals. Their loving spirit would likely want you to share that love with another pet in the future.

2. Consider how your late pet enjoyed the companionship of other animals and how they might have been happy to see you share that love with another furry friend.

3. Imagine what your sweet one would say if they could communicate with you. Trust your intuition and envision their response when contemplating the idea of loving again.

4. Understand that every relationship with a pet is unique and special. Loving another pet doesn't diminish your love for your late companion; it simply opens your heart to new connections and experiences. Each sweet one has a unique personality and a different form of love to give us. Embrace each individual love as time permits you to.

5. Know that your late pet's love is unconditional, and they would want the same love and care for another pet who may need your help and affection.

FINAL THOUGHTS AND MY HEART'S DESIRE FOR YOU

Are you tired? Worn out? Burned out on religion? Come to me. Get away with me and you'll recover your life. I'll show you how to take a real rest. Walk with me and work with me—watch how I do it. Learn the unforced rhythms of grace. I won't lay anything heavy or ill-fitting on you. Keep company with me and you'll learn to live freely and lightly.

MATTHEW 11:28–30, MSG

My beloved, our time together has ended for now, but I'm hoping we will connect again soon! As you continue your healing journey, my heart desires you to rest your mind, body, and spirit, knowing you are loved and blessings are upon you!

You will get through this, my love, because you are stronger than you think, more resilient than you realize, and loved more than you can imagine. You have the perseverance to withstand this season of life you are in. Seasons change, and I declare that you are entering your new season of divine healing, restoration, and peace that surpasses all understanding.

As I mentioned at the beginning of this book, it has been a tremendous honor and pleasure to be on this journey with you. Even though I might not have met you in person yet, we are connected and united in spirit, heart, and love. I pray that, God willing, our paths will meet in person on our journey here on earth.

The good news is that if we don't get a chance to meet in person here on earth, I believe we will meet in heaven one day, celebrating our new life with our sweet ones.

My heart desires for you to know this: we've shared tender moments of vulnerability, understanding, and support. As you move forward, know that you'll always have a true friend here, a beloved friend who understands the depths of sorrow and the tremendous healing power of connection. In spirit, we remain united; in that unity, we find grace, compassion, mercy, loving-kindness, and strength.

And here is one of my favorite Bible verses for you to tuck away and incorporate into your life if you so desire:

> *Summing it all up, friends, I'd say you'll do best by filling your minds and meditating on things true, noble, reputable, authentic, compelling, gracious—the best, not the worst; the beautiful, not the ugly; things to praise, not things to curse. Put into practice what you learned from me, what you heard and saw and realized. Do that, and God, who makes everything work together, will work you into his most excellent harmonies.*
>
> PHILIPPIANS 4:8–9, MSG

Until we meet again, know that you are loved, cherished, adored, valued, victorious, and highly favored because you are a child of the Most High God, who loves you more than you know!

From my heart to yours,

Rachel xoxo

CHAPTER TEN

FOR THOSE WHO ...

FOR THE ESTEEMED VETERINARIANS AND VETERINARY SUPPORT TEAMS

It's a bit challenging for me to know where to begin my love letter to you all. Words cannot express how much you mean to me, our beloved pet parents community, and the individuals who receive your daily loving support, wisdom, encouragement, experience, and dedication to quality care.

The work you do is a calling that touches the hearts of pet parents across the globe.

You dedicate long, sometimes grueling hours, often sacrificing time with your own families, to be on the front lines for my fellow pet parents and me, caring for our sweet ones.

In my role, I often encounter and work with pet parents who are going through various emotions: anger, sadness, and sometimes even despair. Some have faced what they say was a devastating experience with their vet as their cherished companion was being treated for an illness, recovering from a tragic accident, or nearing a peaceful passing through euthanasia.

I can't fully fathom all that you go through. Still, I want you to know that regardless of the specific situations you encounter or the challenges pet parents face, you are valued, respected, honored, and deeply appreciated by me and countless others worldwide.

It weighs heavily on my heart to acknowledge that the veterinary field experiences one of the highest suicide rates in any industry. I believe that not enough people are aware of this grave reality.

I bring this up to let you know that I and many others empathize with your unique struggles while serving and caring for our pets with unwavering dignity and respect. Keep doing what you are doing because you are making a difference. Without a doubt, even though there are some bad apples in any industry, you impact this generation and the next.

I have met countless vets and support teams focused on new treatments and care for the world to benefit from. Thank you for doing all you do.

I hope this letter serves as a heartfelt reminder to you personally of your value. Your work touches lives in ways that words cannot express, and your dedication does not go unnoticed. Thank you, from the depths of my heart, for all you do. If there is anything I can do to support you, let me know.

With boundless gratitude, unwavering
admiration, and from my heart to yours,

Rachel

FOR THOSE WHO ARE ACTIVE MILITARY AND VETERANS WITH K-9 PARTNERS WHO DIED

I don't know any other way to start this letter to you but to say, my beloved friend and hero, my heart is with you, and I hope I am afforded the opportunity and honor of meeting you in person one day.

From a very young age, I remember God placed a special admiration and sense of awe in my heart for our military. I have always supported you and your families with the utmost honor, respect, and admiration possible and will continue to do so for eternity. Your commitment to patriotism, bravery, excellence, selflessness, and humility is noble and inspiring.

I can't imagine what you have experienced and the horrors you have had to encounter. I can't imagine what sacrifices you have had to make that the news or lawmakers don't reveal to the public. And I can't imagine what your families have been through.

Your service and sacrifice in the military demands a level of dedication and courage that few can comprehend. You put your life on the line to protect our nation. Your unwavering commitment to duty and the welfare of your fellow citizens is an inspiration to us all. And accepting the call to keep civilians like me safe and free is something I do not take lightly. Thank you.

Let me be among those who say they are so sorry you've lost your beloved K-9 partner. I can't imagine what it would be like to lose your service animal, your partner, and your best friend who has helped you in war or at home. The bond you experience with your partner is like no other.

I want you to know that my heart aches for your loss. I can only begin to fathom your loyal and devoted companion's profound impact on your life. That bond between you ran uniquely deeper than most people will understand. Your partner was a loyal companion, your confidant, protector, and support system in the face of unimaginable challenges. You faced war trials together, and your bond grew stronger through those shared experiences.

Your loss is a desperately painful experience. They stood by your side through thick and thin, and their absence leaves a void that words cannot fully express. The grief you feel is valid and profound, and giving yourself time and space to mourn this incredible loss is essential, my friend.

In this time of sorrow, please remember you are not alone. As you continue to carry out your noble duties and face the challenges that come your way, remember that your partner's spirit is forever intertwined with yours. Their dedication and skills undoubtedly saved lives and comforted those who served alongside you. Their memory will live on through the stories and the legacy they left behind.

Thank you for your service and sacrifices and for allowing your service dog to be part of your extraordinary journey. May their memory bring you comfort and strength, and may you have peace in your heart knowing that your bravery and selflessness are deeply appreciated and respected.

From my heart to yours,

Rachel

FOR THOSE WHO ARE IN LAW ENFORCEMENT WITH K-9 PARTNERS WHO DIED

The world has changed in so many ways over the recent years. I don't have to point that out because you have experienced this even more than I have.

Since I was very young, I have greatly respected and admired what you have chosen as your life's work, protecting citizens like me and this beautiful country we are so blessed to call home, the United States of America.

For those who are reading this in another beautiful country, I also honor and respect yours, and this love letter is to you, too, my friend. This is for every person who took an oath to protect and serve their community—wherever they are in the world—who has lost their K-9 partners.

Thank you for your bravery, courage, and commitment to make this world better. I can't even begin to imagine the tremendous loss you have experienced in losing your partner. Not just any partner, the one who knew you better than anyone.

Your K-9 partner was your trusted confidant, unwavering support, and guardian on the front lines of duty. They stood by your side through thick and thin, never wavering in their dedication to the mission at hand. They lived out the true meaning of loyalty, and their selflessness inspired us all.

I want you to know that your grief is felt deeply, not only by your fellow law enforcement officers but also by the countless citizens like me who recognize the invaluable service your K-9 partners provided to keep our communities safe.

In the face of adversity and danger, you and your K-9 partner formed an unbreakable bond built on trust and mutual understanding. It takes a special kind of person to forge such a connection with a four-legged friend, and your ability to communicate without words is a testament to your dedication and love for your work.

I want to express my unwavering gratitude for the sacrifices you've made. You put your life on the line daily, trusting that your K-9 partner would protect you just as you protected them. Your bravery is commendable, and your commitment to excellence and serving others sets an example for all of us.

As you mourn the loss of your dear friend and partner, please know that you do not walk this path alone. The law enforcement community and citizens from all walks of life stand with you in solidarity, offering our support and gratitude for your service.

May you find solace in knowing that your K-9 partner's legacy lives on and the bond you shared will remain unbroken. They may no longer be physically present, but their spirit will forever guide and protect you in your noble pursuit of safeguarding our communities.

From my heart to yours,

Rachel

FOR THOSE WHOSE BELOVED
SUPPORT ANIMAL DIED

Your heart must have felt so broken when saying your final goodbye until you meet again in heaven. You have been tremendously blessed to have such a loyal companion by your side.

Losing a beloved support animal is an incredibly painful, and my heart goes out to you during this difficult time. Support animals are special in our hearts, providing comfort, understanding, and companionship. They become more than just pets; they become our confidants and pillars of strength, offering solace during the darkest moments.

The bond between a support animal and its owner is unique and profound. They have been there for you, offering unconditional love and support through life's challenges and helping to ease anxiety, depression, or other emotional burdens. I know their presence brought you a sense of calmness and security that words cannot fully express.

During this time of mourning, surround yourself with understanding and compassionate people who understand the significance of your loss. Seek solace in sharing stories and memories of your sweet one, cherishing the moments that brought joy and happiness into your life.

As you reflect on your time together, know that while they provided you with ample blessings, you provided your support animal with a life filled with love, care, and understanding. They were blessed to have you as their companion, just as you were blessed to have them by your side.

In the midst of sorrow, try to find comfort in knowing that your support animal's spirit will forever be with you. They may not be physically present, but their love and presence will remain etched in your heart and memories. Their impact on your life will continue to shape and guide you, providing strength and courage as you face the days ahead.

As you navigate the grieving process, be kind to yourself and allow yourself the time and space to heal. Embrace the loving support of friends, family, or support groups who can offer understanding and empathy.

May you find peace in knowing that your cherished companion is at peace, and may the memories of your time together bring comfort to your heart. You are not alone in your grief, and as you heal, may you find strength in knowing that your sweet one's spirit will always walk alongside you, guiding you with love and light.

From my heart to yours,

Rachel

FOR THOSE WHOSE PET
DIED IN A TRAGIC ACCIDENT

I don't have enough words or expressions to explain how deeply sorry I am for your loss and how it happened. I can only imagine that you never thought your sweet one would die the way they unfortunately and tragically did.

Losing a beloved pet to a tragic accident is an indescribable pain, and my heart aches for you during this incredibly difficult time.

In moments like these, it's essential to remember the precious memories you shared with your beloved pet. The joyful moments of playfulness and the unconditional love they showered upon you. These memories will forever be in your heart, reminding you of the beautiful life you provided for them.

Feeling overwhelmed with grief and confusion after such an unexpected loss is natural. Remember that there is no right or wrong way to mourn. Allow yourself the time and space to grieve, and lean on your support system for comfort and understanding.

While no words can erase your pain, I hope you find solace in knowing that your pet experienced a life filled with love and care because of you. They knew happiness and warmth through your companionship, and you enriched their life immeasurably.

As you navigate through this grieving process, be gentle with yourself and give yourself permission to heal at your own pace.

In time, the sharpness of this pain may ease, but your beloved pet's love and cherished memories will forever be with you. They may no longer be physically present, but their spirit will always remain a part of your life. May you find strength, healing, and comfort in the love you shared and the beautiful memories that will live on in your heart forever.

From my heart to yours,

Rachel

FOR THOSE WHO HAD TO EUTHANIZE DUE TO FINANCIAL REASONS

For some of you, the title of this devotion may seem strange, but for many others, this is a real-life situation. Having to decide to have your beloved pet euthanized is tragic, and having to decide because you can't afford the medical bills and procedures to keep them alive compounds the devastation.

The agony you must have felt making that decision is more than likely indescribable. I cannot fully express the compassion I feel in the depths of my soul for what you have had to face so that your sweet one would no longer suffer.

One feeling clients often have is the feeling of shame. Shame that they did not have the money to take care of their beloved pet like many people do. That shame runs deep.

My heart goes out to you, beloved, as you carry the weight of this difficult decision made under financial constraints. You are not alone in this struggle; I want you to know there is no shame in facing such a challenging situation. Life is unpredictable, and circumstances beyond our control sometimes force us to make painful choices.

It is essential to recognize that your financial capabilities do not measure your love for your sweet one. The bond you shared with your beloved pet is beyond any material possessions or financial means. Your efforts to care for them and provide love and comfort speak volumes about the depth of your compassion and commitment as a pet owner.

Euthanizing a pet due to financial reasons is an excruciating decision that no one should have to make. But in the face of such hardship, you displayed incredible strength and selflessness, putting your pet's well-being above your own heartache. That act of love is a testament to the beautiful connection you shared with your sweet one.

During this healing time, it's essential to be gentle with yourself. Acknowledge any guilt or shame, but remember that you made the decision with the best intentions in your heart. Allow yourself to grieve and process these emotions. Seek support from understanding friends, family, or even online communities where others have faced similar challenges.

Remember that financial struggles do not define your worth as a person or a pet owner. Life's circumstances can be unpredictable; sometimes, we find ourselves in difficult positions despite our best efforts. In these trying times, practicing self-forgiveness and giving yourself permission to heal is crucial.

Please remember that your love for your sweet one endures, and your shared memories will always remain in your heart. Take time to heal, and know you are not alone on this journey. May you find solace in knowing that you did your best and that your actions were driven by love and compassion.

From my heart to yours,

Rachel

FOR THOSE WHO HAD TO EUTHANIZE DUE TO BEHAVIORAL ISSUES

My heart is with you! I have been on the other end of the phone when you called, distraught, disillusioned, and heartbroken, knowing this was your last option for the safety of your sweet one and those around them.

Many people don't realize this is a compassionate ending of life, preventing devastating and inevitable outcomes. But you, my beloved friend, know this truth firsthand. What you have endured while making this decision is something no one ever wants to imagine.

It's important to acknowledge that euthanizing due to dangerous behavior is a decision that stems from deep love and concern for the well-being of both your sweet one and those around them. Putting the safety of others first is a sign of your responsibility and compassion as a pet owner.

While it is natural to wonder about "what ifs" and to question whether you could have done anything differently, please be gentle with yourself. Hindsight can be cruel, but remember that you made the best decision with the information and resources available to you at the time. Sometimes, despite our best efforts, circumstances can be beyond our control.

I want you to know that no one has the right to judge you, your family, your vet's recommendation, your trainer's recommendation, or any other person contributing to your decision.

You did the best you could with the information you had. You are not alone. Countless families have experienced what you have. The details might be a bit different, but the torment in your heart, the sleepless nights, the endless crying, and the relief that your sweet one was able to have a peaceful and compassionate passing connect you.

You were a good steward to your sweet one. But unfortunately, we can never know what an animal's behavior will ultimately be. They are still wild animals in their instincts.

Yes, we have domesticated them, but that does not guarantee they will not be aggressive in nature and harm those they love. Sometimes, all the love, affection, care, and discipline we offer will not be enough to change their aggressive nature.

Remember, you know the truth of your situation and circumstances. God was with you in your decision-making, and He is with you now, encouraging you to have hope and faith you will see your sweet one again in heaven. They are with God, healed, whole, and ready to love you again when you're in heaven with them.

I invite you to release any guilt, shame, remorse, and resentment right now in this very moment. But don't ever downplay the significance of doing everything in your power to help your sweet one overcome their aggressive nature.

You are a good person who had to make one of the most complex decisions in the world. Always remember that this difficult decision does not define you. This experience does not diminish your capacity for love and care.

Allow yourself to heal, forgive yourself, and find comfort in knowing you did what you believed was best for your beloved companion. In time, as you heal, try to remember the joyous moments and the love you shared with your sweet one. Cherish the memories of the happy times, the tail wags, and the cuddles. Know that you provided a loving home and did everything possible to give them a good life.

As you continue your healing journey, consider honoring your sweet one's memory in the most meaningful way. This could be through creating a memorial, supporting animal welfare causes, or even opening your heart to another needy pet when you feel ready.

If your heart needs healing from this traumatic event, I suggest you find others who have been through what you have. Nothing is more healing than hearing, "I understand how you feel because I have been right where you are."

My heart is with you, my beloved friend. From my heart to yours,

Rachel

FOR THOSE WHO DO NOT HAVE CHILDREN

Having children is a blessing for those who believe it is a blessing. And some of us may believe it's a blessing but don't have any of our own for various reasons.

Unfortunately, childless individuals and couples are often looked down upon as though something is wrong with us. The judgment on people's faces when they learn someone doesn't have kids is obvious most of the time. I'm not casting everyone into this generalization, but many people judge and jump to assumptions when encountering a childless adult.

Whether it was your choice not to have children, your health would not allow it to happen, you terminated a pregnancy, or any other reason, the reason and the feelings associated with it are your business between you, God, and your loved ones.

As I said previously, we are created to be nurturers—whether to our own children, other people's children (as educators, coaches, therapists, pediatric physicians, spiritual aunts and uncles, etc.), or our pets.

In fact, there is something extraordinary about knowing that you have a purpose in caring for and nurturing your pet, one of the most profound relationships in the world (and no doubt unlike any human relationship you've had). Indeed, the world can't figure us out, but God can, and He has paid us double for our trouble! We get to live a life full of joy caring for His beautiful creatures.

You may not understand why it wasn't in God's will for you to have human children, and you may even have a lot of hard feelings about that, but as with any kind of grief, these unanswered questions require acceptance to find peace.

Being a pet parent is how God wanted me to parent. I'm glad I accepted His call. He calls us all to care for this planet, all of His creatures, and for other humans because His creation is precious to Him. We are just among the fortunate to have been pet parents.

I know you are devastated by the loss of your beloved pet. My heart is with you. I experienced the same heartache as you. I promise you, my love that you will get through this. It will be a journey requiring your patience and belief that God has the best in store for you as His child, but you will get there. So keep on keeping on, my beloved friend; hold your head up high, and remember, you are loved, valued, cherished, and highly favored!

You will see your sweet one again in heaven!

From my heart to yours,

Rachel

FOR THOSE WHO HAVE
CHILDREN THAT ARE
MOURNING TOO

Many families I'm honored to work with have children in the home trying to understand why their beloved pet and best friend had to die. It's a complicated conversation in any situation, but it's especially challenging if the death was unexpected for them.

I want you to know that you are an incredible parent, and you and your family will get through this because of your leadership in the grieving process.

I'm often asked about resources for helping children navigate the grief of a pet. Child development experts say children's literature is a fantastic outlet for explaining complex situations, like grief and exploring feelings. Thankfully, many wonderful children's books help you facilitate family conversations about death, emotions, and grief.

I recommend you visit the library or purchase a few on Amazon to get these conversations started creatively and sensitively. I'm confident that these books will be an incredible tool for you to help your child work through their questions and feelings in their time of loss.

As you read those children's books together, take the opportunity to discuss their feelings, helping them process their feelings and make sense of the loss. Sometimes, children may have questions about death and what happens afterward. Be honest with them and be sensitive to their age and maturity level, tailoring your explanations accordingly.

My heart is with you as you navigate through the grief, grow in your strength as a family, and memorialize the pet you all so dearly loved. With perseverance, thoughtfulness, grace, and love, you and your family will be just fine in time.

Remember, being patient with your children during this time of mourning is essential. Just as I've been encouraging you, let them know that it's okay to feel a wide range of emotions and that there's no right or wrong way to grieve. Encourage open communication and create a safe space—metaphorically and even physically, if possible—to help them express their feelings freely.

Consider setting up a small memorial for your beloved pet, like a photo collage, a butterfly garden, or even planting a tree in their honor. This can be a comforting way for the whole family to come together and remember the joy and love your sweet one brought into your lives.

And remember, it's okay for you as a parent to grieve as well and for your child to see it. They are actually looking to you for how they can healthily work through hard things. Your beautiful children need to see that grieving is a natural process and that taking care of yourself emotionally and physically is crucial.

Seek support from friends, family, or a grief counselor if needed. You can lean on each other for strength and find comfort in sharing your memories of your cherished pet.

Your family will come out stronger from this experience, and the lessons learned through grief and loss will shape the compassion and resilience of your children as they grow.

Always remind your children that their beloved sweet one will forever hold a special place in their hearts and that the love they shared will continue to live on in their cherished memories. Don't be afraid to talk openly about treasured memories. Though it's tough now, they will look back with a smile on the joy and happiness their pet brought into their lives.

Above all, be kind to yourselves and allow each family member to grieve in their own unique way and time. Remember that healing is a process; taking all the time you need is okay.

May your family find comfort in one another's love and support during this difficult time and emerge from this experience with even stronger bonds and resilience. Take time to remember cherished memories, stay creative in honoring your sweet one, and celebrate the life once lived because it was all worth it in the end.

From my heart to yours,

Rachel

CHAPTER ELEVEN

CLIENT STORIES IN THEIR OWN WORDS

ANNE AND CHARLIE'S STORY
IN ANNE'S OWN WORDS

Charlie came into my life when I was young, single, and carefree. It had been over a decade since my beloved childhood dog, Eva, had passed, so I felt ready. I did not realize at the time, though, how much of an impact this lively, four-and-a-half pound, snuffling, furry-faced beagle puppy would have on me for the next sixteen years.

I got him when he was nine weeks old, but I didn't get married until he was twelve years old, so it was just the two of us for a long time. He was my light, my center, my family.

Charlie was with me for every milestone. He was by my side in the hospice when my mom died, he spent holidays with me, and he inspired me to quit my economic policy job mid-career and apply to vet school.

We traveled cross-country together, spent vacations together, and moved into my first home together. We shared moments that many experience with a partner or a family. He adjusted to life when our family expanded to include my husband, and then again when I welcomed my daughter into the world.

This merry little hound was also a big part of my day-to-day. He was the first and last one I would see. Giddy with excitement, I would wake up and run downstairs to greet him. It felt like Christmas morning, every morning.

He patiently waited for me on the days when I worked long hours and the weeks when my job required longer trips to Africa, Europe, and India. When I changed careers and started working back-to-back shifts at the emergency animal hospital, he obliged to the change in routine with no complaints. And he dutifully followed me to California when I became a student again. He even became fond of jogging alongside me on the beach (beagles generally don't like water, and this beagle usually reveled in his off-leash freedom). He indulged me as I shot every possible angle of "beach beagle" with his long ears flapping in the wind.

I took him everywhere I could. I snuck him into stores, pools, and even fancy brunches in Malibu. One time he charmed the tow truck driver and convinced him to give my sister, himself, and me a ride in the cab when my car broke down on one of the coldest days in DC. "No dogs allowed" didn't compute.

Charlie was game for all of it. I would be lying if I didn't confess to doting on this dog. He quickly became accustomed to doggie daycare, stays at a pet resort, canine birthday parties, and beagle meet ups.

It didn't help when Uno, the first beagle to win the Westminster Dog Show, became world-famous in 2008. Charlie capitalized on his celebrity status after being repeatedly stopped on the street and asked if he was Uno. You would have thought he was the one who had won the title.

Because of their strong sense of smell, beagles are notorious for getting into trouble when left unsupervised, and Charlie was no exception. He was a master at swiping unattended food off of coffee tables, especially at Thanksgiving.

He wasn't as discriminating as one would expect either. Inedible items were up for grabs as well. Rocks, nails, coins. It didn't matter. Vet visits did not deter him. He did not understand consequences, as my mother used to say. He had a penchant for socks. No sock was safe in the house. He could cram three into his mouth at one time, and if you ever tried to negotiate and trade a treat for a sock, he managed to grab the treat while keeping the socks. He became quite skilled at unpacking suitcases.

Six months into the pandemic, after my daughter had just turned one,

Charlie was diagnosed with cutaneous lymphoma, an aggressive form of skin cancer. The vet gave him 2–6 months to live, depending on the course of treatment. I felt like I had been punched in the gut.

I spent the next several months educating myself about the disease, exploring treatment options, reading clinical studies, and figuring out how to give him the best care possible during COVID.

I elected to try chemotherapy, since the most effective drug for his type of cancer was generally well-tolerated by dogs with minimal side effects. And for the first six months, Charlie remained his fun-loving, table-swiping, sock-stealing, mischievous self.

We included him in every family activity, and I took a leave of absence to spend his remaining months together. By my daughter's second birthday in April, however, he was clearly declining.

The treatments had become less effective, his behavior was changing, and his appetite was not as robust. I spent the next two months agonizing over when to put an end to his life. He still had many good days, and he wasn't suffering—at least so I thought—but I was terrified.

I didn't want to let him go. He was supposed to watch my daughter grow up. What if he started to turn the corner, and I acted too soon? Ending this faithful little companion's life was unimaginable.

There is no right time. You make the best decision with the information that you have at the time. It has taken me two years to give myself this grace. I said goodbye to my best friend on June 20, 2021, Father's Day. He was one month shy of his seventeenth birthday.

I am no stranger to loss, but this loss was more profound. Charlie had been there for me during so many periods of intense grief; I felt overwhelmed by the prospect of having to grieve him alone. I had never needed him as much as I did now.

I am immensely grateful for the guidance and grace that Rachel Shirley provided me. She helped me adjust to a new normal as Charlie's death slowly became a reality.

She gave me something to hold on to when I felt depleted and disoriented as I shifted between denial and acceptance in the months just after his passing. Later on, anniversaries, holidays, and other important milestones were a little easier to navigate with her support.

I first spoke to Rachel five days after Charlie passed. I will never forget her kind, gentle voice on the phone as I tried to put into words my loss that was still so raw. She provided a safe space for me to mourn.

She suggested coping strategies that I could put to use immediately. She comforted me when I was having a particularly challenging day, but gave me space to "stretch," as she would say, and grow on the days when I was ready to take a step that moved me slightly out of my comfort zone. She was particularly skilled at picking up on my cues and providing gentle nudging when needed.

When I asked Rachel for additional support resources, she did not hesitate to refer me to other helpful resources and a colleague who is a pet loss counselor. They taught me that there is no timeline for grief. Grief is unpredictable. It never goes away, but it changes. It's not linear. It's something that you process in pieces, and it can help to visualize it as something that is experienced in waves.

When I felt rushed, Rachel would gently remind me of how long Charlie and I were together—in days—to emphasize that I should not expect the intensity of my grief to subside immediately.

They helped me come up with ways to honor him, his memory, and the people who cared for him and loved him. It has not only been healing for me but has also taught me how to model a healthy way to grieve to my daughter.

We talk about Charlie as a family all of the time. We look at photos and retell the same stories, recalling all of his antics. My daughter feels safe saying that she misses Charlie. The support system I had in place highlighted and pointed out all of the lessons that this little dog has given me.

He has taught me how to live mindfully and to be present for my daughter, and how to be a better mother. He taught me how to forgive. He taught me about the reality of loss. He taught me about compassion. I can honor him by incorporating these lessons into my life.

They made me feel heard and less alone in a society that does not fully acknowledge pet loss and at a time when much of the world was already experiencing tremendous upheaval in the middle of COVID.

They never complained when I repeated the same stories. And they continued to listen, without judgment, when almost everyone else had moved on. They validated my feelings by letting me know that it is okay to be sad.

They also reminded me of ways to feel joy. I have to admit that this is still an area in progress. But I'm working on redefining joy and recognizing that it might come in a different form.

It has been two years since I lost Charlie. I miss him every single day. But, I am trying to appreciate that the sadness I still feel is a reflection of the immense love I will always have for him.

—Anne A.

MIA AND BONNIE'S STORY
IN MIA'S OWN WORDS

My sweet Bonnie's passing was very sudden. There was no time for anticipatory grief. There was so much love between us left to share.

Ten years ago, my life was about to change the moment I walked through the animal shelter door, and it was love at first sight when I saw the most adorable, sweet little black toy poodle with big brown eyes who was sitting on the welcome counter, and immediately, our eyes met. It was as if this little dog said through her eyes, "I'm yours, Mommy." Bonnie was two years old. I immediately wanted to take her home. They told me someone would come later that day to take her but they would call me if they did not come. My friend and I went to dinner and both had our phones on the table waiting anxiously for it to ring. She was all we could talk about. At the end of the day, I got the call. Bonnie was mine. I couldn't believe the happiness and immense joy that I was experiencing. It was too late in the day to take her home so I had to return the next day.

I was 60 years old and never had a dog, let alone any pet. I had no idea how to prepare. When the shelter took the adoption photo, I didn't even know how to hold her. Bonnie was so small in my arms. That night she slept next to me on the bed, and in the morning, I knew exactly what to do and how to take care of her. She made it easy. Bonnie melted my heart and brought years of incredible joy and contentment into my life. We were inseparable. My friends would say they never saw me without Bonnie. I never felt lonely with her by my side.

Bonnie was such a special girl. Everyone told me so. She went everywhere with me even when I traveled across the country to work. We did everything together. She would be on my lap or walking next to me. Bonnie was so tiny that she fit right in my arm as I walked around the house. Bonnie loved to take long walks and would keep walking even when I was tired and ready to go home.

I had the honor and pleasure of fostering children for many years. Being a parent and adding value to these wonderful kids made life fulfilling, and it was even more so when Bonnie joined the family. When a child in distress was brought to my home—usually in the middle of the night—Bonnie would sleep with them. She knew who needed her most.

When she looked into my eyes, I felt loved, appreciated, admired, valued, and loved unconditionally. What more could a person ask for?

Bonnie passed away during COVID, so I could not go into the vet's office with her to see the doctors. We went to an oncologist and were sitting in the car when the doctor stood behind the window looking at us sadly, shaking her head while I held Bonnie. There was nothing more that could be done to help her.

We only had two weeks together after I received Bonnie's diagnosis. One day, she began retreating under the bed for hours at a time when she always slept curled up next to me. I put a soft blanket for her on the floor. I spent those weeks in bed so I could always be near her.

I cherish the last photo of us together. Bonnie was sitting at the end of the bed looking into my eyes, and I felt she was saying something to me. I was looking deeply back into her big brown eyes and I understood.

On our last evening together, I was outside and Bonnie was sitting on the grass. Then, a rainbow appeared and I told her that it was for her.

The next day while I was on the bed, I heard Bonnie very slowly coming out from under the bed, and she was walking to the side of the bed that I was on. As she came around the corner, I jumped up off the bed and went to her. As I picked her up, she went limp in my arms. I knew she was gone.

With her last breath, Bonnie came to me to die in my arms. In retrospect, it was a blessed end to our time together. She cared for me so much and wanted her transition to be a beautiful moment.

It has been over three years since I lost my precious Bonnie. Through those painful days, and when the grief is unbearable, Rachel has been a great support throughout my grieving process. The first few sessions all I did was cry for the hour and she just listened and was always there for me. She is still helping me through this journey.

I think of Bonnie every day, and the grief and loss feel palpable.

Bonnie is forever in my heart.

—Mia

TIM'S AND KEELY'S STORY IN TIM'S OWN WORDS

Dear Keely,

Before I commit another word to paper, I must express this: I miss you. So very much. It is a longing with no end. A persistent ache where my heart reaches out for you, and you're just out of my grasp.

Yet somehow, in the same breath, you remain with me, beside me, inside me, never far away. This is the sometimes maddening duality of grief.

It's been said that "every new beginning comes from some other beginning's end." After I lost my beloved childhood dog, Toby, at fifteen, I was very resistant for years to the idea of getting another companion. It hurt too much. It felt disloyal to my best buddy. But a dog lover is typically a dog lover soul-deep. After eight years, I was ready for you.

Our beginning was memorable. Discovering you, the runt of the litter, the last puppy to need a home, tucked away on a farm in rural northern Minnesota. You stood on your back legs and reached up as I gazed at you over the barn railing. Love at first sight.

Your personality was unforgettable. You were always so engaged and agreeable, but you also made crystal clear what you did or didn't want. You were so gentle with humans and animals alike, but not with me when I provoked you into one of our legendary wrestling battles.

You exulted in the outdoors. Even if I was stepping out for a moment, you were at my side, whether it was frolicking in the sunshine, crunching through leaves, or bounding through the snow. You lived for our adventurous walks in the woods. You didn't walk; you pranced.

You were fearless as you jumped an entire flight of stairs in one leap. You were glee personified when a new toy arrived with a new squeaker to disable instantly. You broke apart the old stereotype by actually loving our mail deliveries.

Your exuberant greetings every time you were reunited with me, my Mom, Debbie, or my sister Kelsey made us feel like the most important people on earth.

And let us not forget the food. All dogs have an affinity for chowing down, but you turned it into an art form, Keely Pie.

You stared so intensely at your humans that they couldn't even fathom feasting before you got your portion. You truly experienced food; it remains my finest culinary compliment ever received when I cooked my crispy ranch chicken, and you licked the pan until I worried about the survival of its non-stick coating.

You knew us so well that even small mood changes triggered your concern. And when we were really struggling, you were the glue that held us together.

I'll never forget your piercing gaze of concern to the point that you trembled after I returned home with a pulled tooth. You always licked it all better. How many tears did you kiss away in your glorious life? It's often stated we take care of our pets. I argue that they much more frequently take care of us.

Endings are hinted at even when we don't wish to see them. It broke my heart the first time I embarked on a longer walk without you, as your worsening arthritis wouldn't allow you to. You stood in the window and barked, not comprehending how I could go without you.

Vet visits became more frequent. You loved Dr. K and his team, not so much any poking, prodding, or dreaded nail clipping.

Yet you aged so gracefully, baby girl. Your puppy enthusiasm for the day never ceased. You savored our jaunts around the block and yard every bit as much as you embraced our long walks. You lived life on your terms and let nothing diminish your journey. You never stopped infusing our lives with love, joy, and light.

I don't often think of your stroke and its devastating aftermath. What are six days compared to a decade and a half of blessings?

We tried to comfort you and remind you we were there. Whispering over and over how loved you were, that you were such a good girl, that it's okay to rest now. Your final gift will remain with me until the day I am no more in this world and join you in the next.

Mom was driving to the vet. With fluid entering your lungs, it was time to bring you the peace you richly deserved. I held you tightly in my arms, feeling utterly vacant.

We were moments away when a wave of complete and total calm caressed me. I've tried to put the sensation into words countless times, and they remain lacking. At the most devastating moment of my life, I was gifted a peace that surpassed all understanding. I know your soul went home at that moment.

I carried you inside, resting you on an exam table. Dr. K. entered, checked your vitals, and said, "Guys, she's already gone." Mom, Kels, and I erupted in tears.

I firmly believe to this day that you departed the world in my arms to save us from having to make the inevitable choice as your last loving act.

The first day without you was torment. I howled with abandon, feeling like I was dying. Darkness enveloped my being. The silence of a home absent from your life was deafening, suffocating.

My support system couldn't be fully called upon as they were struggling and bereft right along with me. Though I was immeasurably blessed by several loved ones' efforts and support, I knew I needed to reach out for specialized help.

Four days after losing you, Rachel came into my life.

Instantly a source of limitless empathy, sincerity, and wisdom, Rachel reminded me how crucial it was to take care of myself. To know that some days would be consumed with despair while others would contain small gems of hope. The key was to let it all be felt and acknowledged.

Our Zoom groups were invaluable in connecting me with others suffering from losing their animals and searching for a way forward. Being able to be completely honest about my emotions and setbacks, and to celebrate even minor victories began to salve the wounds of your absence.

Tributes to you hurt but also helped. I cried the first time I made your chicken without you. I wept, tracing your trails in the woods while sprinkling some of your ashes, ensuring part of you will always dwell where you were happiest.

Tears watered the grass before me as I gazed at your gravestone.

Yet all of these acts and many to come were and are done to honor you and your impact on me and all who knew and loved you.

People often see life as a series of beginnings and ends. But the more I think about it, what counts more than anything is what endures.

The lessons you taught me endure, Keely. Let everyone know how much you love them as big as you can. Every. Single. Day. Embrace each day with excitement, hope, expectation, and anticipation. You showed me that when circumstances keep you from doing what you once did, do the next best thing with just as much passion. Open your heart to everyone. Forgive fast. Savor every bite.

You illustrated to me that if I hadn't opened my heart once more I'd have missed out on a life shared with you that blessed us so. Thanks to you, I know without hesitation that I will one day love another dog when I'm ready, though you can never and will never be replaced.

You illuminated the fact that one's soulmate can be a canine, as the love, trust, adoration, patience, and tireless dependability you personified is rare indeed to find in most people.

The gifts your life brought me also endure. Mom and I visit Dr. Kalinoski, Luann, Bobbie, and the compassionate team at the Mesaba Animal Hospital with treats and hugs every now and again. They cherished you and fought for you; they are family for life. So is Rachel, who remains a dear friend whom I love and admire deeply. She's given so much of herself to so many, and I know her words and light will inspire, touch, guide, and heal many through this book.

Grief is enduring, too. I write this two years and one month after your loss. Some days, I'm aglow with memories and images of you. On other days, those exact same things crush me.

Grief is not linear; it's a circle we find ourselves in different sectors of day to day. Grief isn't a phase; it's a new part of us that we need to learn to co-exist with always. Grief is a highway we are all travelers on; we're just at different junctures.

But what endures most of all? My love for you, Keely. You are with me for eternity, as much a part of me as the matter I consist of. My longing also endures and always will until the day I cross the bridge that briefly separates us and race to you.

Thank you for choosing me as your best friend, brother, walker, chef, toy thrower, sparring partner, caretaker, and father. I'll see you when it's time, and I hope this and all I do the rest of my days make you proud.

Until then, rest well, my dear girl.

Love,

Tim

ACKNOWLEDGMENTS

This written compilation of love letters for pet loss parents, from my heart to theirs, would not have been possible without the unwavering belief in my message, mission, and ministry of my family, friends, clients, and writing partners.

My Mother, Deborah, whose unlimited loving support helped guide me through embarking on this journey, was my guiding light as she championed me along the finish line. She introduced me to horses, my first love, and filled my life growing up with beautiful horses, dogs, and cats, and for that, I am forever grateful. My Mother-in-Love, Barbara, has been my biggest cheerleader and fan since day one, and it's so much fun being her shining star.

My Father, Warren, who started the development of my faith journey, took me to church as a little girl, took me to the barn every day after school so I could ride my horse, and taught me what having a loving Father is like. And to my stepfather, Marty, whose unconditional love, support, and encouragement continue to shape the person I am today and becoming.

Without the foundation my loving parents gave me, I would not be the person I am today, and for that, I am eternally grateful.

Thank you to my loving husband, Simon, whose steadfast belief and love for me resonates with everything I do. Simon, you are the one who gently reminded me never to allow critics to steal my joy and destiny, and for that, I am grateful.

Thank you to my writing partners whose vision, wisdom, and experience I leaned on as they encouraged me to be all God intended.

My dear friend Carolyn at Carolyn Reed Consulting, I cannot express my gratitude for your unwavering belief, faith, and dedication to each project I have presented to you over the years. Your ability to instantly take my vision into conception and completion is priceless. Every day, I thank our Heavenly Father for divinely connecting us to make an impact on the Kingdom.

Thank you to those who helped me on my publishing journey, including Amber Parr Burdett for your exceptional editorial contribution, Steve Kuhn for your superior formatting and interior design of this book, and @_.augustosilva._ for beautifully capturing my message with your cover design. Thank you to Krissy Nelson with Krissy Nelson Ministries for your tremendous encouragement, supportive coaching, and valuable expertise.

And last but not least, thank you to my beloved boxer boys Winston, Spencer, and Charley. Thank you for loving me so well and enriching my life more significantly than I imagined. I promised you to write this book to support your fellow furry friend's human parents as they eagerly await their reunion with them in heaven. Don't worry, I'm not done supporting them and have many more books to write…

NOTES

CHAPTER ONE

1. James W. Skehan, *Place Me With Your Son: Ignatian Spirituality in Everyday Life*, 3rd ed. (Washington, D.C.: Georgetown University Press, 1991), 24.

2. Randy Alcorn, *Heaven: A Comprehensive Guide to What the Bible Says About Our Eternal Home* (Carol Stream: Tyndale Momentum, 2004), 383.

CHAPTER TWO

3. Elisabeth Kubler Ross, *Death: The Final Stage of Growth* (New York: Touchstone Book, 1997), 96.

4. *Oxford Languages Online*, accessed November 22, 2023, https://www.google.com/search?sca_esv=5 83420096&rlz=1C1RXQR_enUS1081US1081&q=transparent&si=ALGXSlYpmWhtmlIZKYHTCPXiY mME-nLIcagLtkxK3zWUCsvkRK90ujEpIyu7BH4oSpv89XVsUc_mQarhEMmu39uccdY4LKxApDF AgmzBE1DwyF_4ZUzVH0w%3D&expnd=1&sa=X&ved=2ahUKEwjryeSfgMyCAxX8HUQIHbRICt EQ2v4IegUIDxDCAQ&biw=1280&bih=675&dpr=1.5

5. Elisabeth Kubler Ross, *Death: The Final Stage of Growth* (New York: Touchstone Book, 1997), 96.

CHAPTER THREE

6. Alan D. Wolfelt, *You're Not Crazy—You're Grieving: 6 Steps for Surviving Loss* (Fort Collins: Companion Press, 2023), 2.

7. Mark Twain, *The Devil's Race-Track: Mark Twain's 'Great Dark' Writings* (Berkeley: University of California Press, 2005), 52.

8. Martin Luther, *AZQuotes*, accessed September 3, 2023. https://www.azquotes.com/quote/590511

9. Elizabeth Barrett Browning, *AZQuotes*, accessed September 3, 2023, https://www.azquotes.com/quote/598851.

CHAPTER FOUR

10. Alex MacLean, *Grave Situation*, (2014).

11. Elisabeth Kubler-Ross, *EKR Foundation*, accessed September 2, 2023, https://www.ekrfoundation.org/elisabeth-kubler-ross/quotes/.

12. Matthew Kelley, *Do Something Beautiful for God: The Essential Teachings of Mother Teresa 365 Daily Reflections* (North Palm Beach, FL: Blue Sparrow Books, 2019), Oct 15.

CHAPTER FIVE

13. Brittin Oakman, Instagram.com/B.Oakman, post on December 20, 2016, accessed September 2, 2023.

14. Alan D. Wolfelt, *When Your Pet Dies: A Guide to Mourning, Remembering, and Healing* (Companion Press, 2004).

15. Alejandra Vasquez, "How to Practice Self-Care While Grieving: Step by Step," *Cake*, April 29, 2022, https://www.joincake.com/blog/self-care-and-grief

16. Maya Angelou. Goodreads.com, accessed September 3, 2023 https://www.goodreads.com/quotes/519946-without-courage-we-cannot-practice-any-other-virtue-with-consistency

17. Joyce Meyer, *Healing the Soul of a Woman Devotional: 90 Inspirations for Overcoming Your Emotional Wounds* (New York: Hachette Books, 2019), 106.

CHAPTER SIX

18. Earl A. Grollman, *Straight Talk About Death for Teenagers: How to Cope with Losing Someone You Love* (Boston: Beacon Press, 2014), 6.

19. Henry Longfellow, *The Complete Prose Works of Longfellow with His Later Poems* (New York: Boston Houghton, Mifflin and Company, 1883), 1196.

20. David Kessler, Grief.com, accessed September 2, 2023, https://grief.com/grief-quotes-memes/grief-is-work-avoiding-grief-quote-by-david-kessler-11/.

CHAPTER SEVEN

21. Bruce F. Singer, *Black Duck Moments Every Day: Daily Affirmations for Chronic Pain and Chronic Illness* (Danbury: Forty Acres and a Mountain Publishing), 236.

22. Caron B. Goode & Tara Paterson, *Raising Intuitive Children: Guide Your Children to Know and Trust Their Gifts* (Pompton Plains: New Page Books, 2009), 6.

23. Mitch Albom, *The Five People You Meet in Heaven* (New York: Hyperion, 2003), 173.

24. John Bate, *A Cyclopaedia of Illustrations of Moral and Religious Truths* (London: Wesleyan Conference Center, 1865), 782.

CHAPTER EIGHT

25. Leonard Sweet, Twitter.com, post on June 6, 2013, accessed September 3, 2023, https://twitter.com/lensweet/status/342588038267957248.

26. Joel Osteen, Facebook.com post on November 14, 2013, accessed on September 3, 2023, https://www.facebook.com/JoelOsteen/posts/10153550059365227.

27. Booker T. Washington, *Up from Slavery: An Autobiography* (New York: Doubleday, Page & Co., 1907), 66.

28. Mother Teresa, GoodReads.com, accessed September 3, 2023, https://www.goodreads.com/quotes/338677-one-truly-must-have-suffered-oneself-to-help-others

29. Reinhold Niebuhr, Serenity prayer (1933).

CHAPTER NINE

30. Eleanor Roosevelt, *You Learn by Living* (Louisville: Westminster John Knox Press, 1960), Foreword.

31. Richard Puz, *The Carolinian* (2009)

32. The Billy Graham Library, "10 Quotes from Billy Graham on Grief", September 6, 2019, https://billygrahamlibrary.org/blog-10-quotes-from-billy-graham-on-grief/.

33. Lakesidefuneralhomega.com, accessed September 2, 2023. https://www.lakesidefuneralhomega.com/7-uplifting-quotes-about-letting-go-after-a-loss

Made in the USA
Middletown, DE
19 March 2024

51248890R00142